BAC 94

Anglais

Sujets 93

CORRIGÉS

Jean-Jacques PEDUSSAUD

BORDAS

© Bordas, Paris, 1993
ISBN 2-04-020918-2

SOMMAIRE

■ CONSEILS PRÉLIMINAIRES

L'épreuve écrite d'anglais se décompose en trois parties distinctes et en principe indépendantes (voir plus loin pour la production guidée) auxquelles on répond en général directement sur la copie prévue à cet effet :
A. Compétence linguistique.
B. Compréhension d'un texte de trente à quarante lignes.
C. Production écrite (deux essais).
Chacune des trois parties fait appel à des compétences particulières ; les candidats doivent donc s'entraîner **régulièrement aux trois types d'exercice.**

A. COMPÉTENCE LINGUISTIQUE

Il est vivement conseillé de commencer par cette partie qui demande une certaine disponibilité d'esprit, avant donc de s'être plongé dans le texte ou dans les sujets de production écrite. Compter environ une demi-heure.

Cette partie est sans doute celle à laquelle il est le plus facile de s'entraîner par un travail systématique, les exercices étant très répétitifs.

Elle peut couvrir des compétences aussi bien lexicales ou phonétiques que proprement grammaticales. On constate d'ailleurs depuis quelques années, une augmentation de fréquence des exercices portant sur le vocabulaire et la prononciation.

Il s'agit de 4 à 8 (en général 5 ou 6) petits exercices séparés qui peuvent prendre les formes suivantes :
– questionnaire à choix multiples (QCM) ;
– exercice lacunaire (blancs à remplir) ;
– exercice d'assortiment (mots ou tronçons de phrases à raccorder) ;
– groupes de mots dans le désordre à remettre dans l'ordre pour former une phrase cohérente ;
– exercices de reformulation :
  - à partir du français,
  - à partir de l'anglais : phrases à raccorder par un mot de liaison, phrase à l'actif à mettre au passif, discours direct à mettre au discours indirect, reformulation à partir d'une amorce de phrase, etc. ;
– traduction d'un membre de phrase (modaux) ;
– éléments à assortir (synonymes notamment) ;
– reconnaître la syllabe portant l'accent tonique ;
– autres exercices portant sur la prononciation.

Pour les QCM, dans le doute, procéder par élimination. C'est le résultat qui compte, peu importe la méthode employée pour y parvenir. Soyez pragmatique !

Obligez-vous à toujours répondre à toutes les questions ; une question sans réponse comptant comme une réponse erronée, vous ne pouvez pas y perdre de points (sauf cas extrêmement rares).

B. COMPRÉHENSION DE L'ÉCRIT

Cette partie se subdivise généralement en compréhension globale et compréhension détaillée, voire approfondie (reconnaître les enjeux implicites du texte). Compter environ une heure.

Commencer par lire le texte posément. Le lire plusieurs fois et ne pas hésiter à faire des diagrammes au brouillon pour symboliser le lieu, la structure temporelle s'il s'agit d'un récit, les personnages et leurs relations entre eux (familiales, affectives ou professionnelles). Cela peut paraître absurde mais il n'est pas toujours facile de démêler qui est qui dans un fragment de roman pris hors contexte. Lorsque le texte comporte des dialogues, il peut être utile de souligner les répliques de chaque personnage de couleurs différentes. Attention aux surlignages qui rendent l'autre côté de la feuille illisible !

Lire l'ensemble des questions en entier avant d'y répondre (éventuellement, commencer à répondre au crayon à papier et ne pas oublier de repasser ensuite à l'encre !). En effet, les questions de la fin peuvent parfois donner la réponse de certaines questions du début. Revenir ensuite aux passages difficiles et ne pas hésiter à les relire autant de fois qu'il le faut. Vous pouvez remarquer tout à coup un détail que vous aviez négligé lors d'une première lecture.

Les questions peuvent prendre les formes suivantes :
– *right or wrong, true or false* avec ou sans justification à apporter par des citations du texte (si on vous le demande, c'est essentiel ; vous serez pénalisé si vous ne citez pas) ;
– QCM portant sur le ton, le lieu, la date, les personnages, leur point de vue ou celui du narrateur (qui n'est pas nécessairement le même) ;
– compréhension de certaines expressions idiomatiques du texte (à partir d'une expression donnée, trouver son synonyme ou son contraire dans le texte) ;
– version : traduction d'un court passage tiré du texte ;
– thème : traduction en anglais de phrases idiomatiques en rapport avec le texte.

Garder pour la fin les questions portant sur le ton du texte, même si elles sont posées au début. En effet l'étude détaillée peut s'avérer éclairante en la matière. D'autre part, c'est souvent **la fin** du texte qui détermine le ton de l'ensemble. Dans le doute, privilégiez donc le ton des deux ou trois derniers paragraphes.

Les justifications des *right or wrong* ou les synonymes/antonymes à repérer apparaissent souvent dans le texte dans l'ordre où sont posées les questions. On vous précisera d'ailleurs souvent : ordre chronologique (ordre du texte) ou ordre non-chronologique (dans le désordre).

Pour les synonymes/antonymes les donner si possibles à la même forme grammaticale que le mot fourni (ex. : base verbale ou forme -*ING* s'il s'agit d'un verbe).

C. PRODUCTION ÉCRITE

Il s'agit de **deux** rédactions consécutives. Les mêmes exigences de base s'appliquent que pour une dissertation en français : **respecter le sujet** et produire un texte cohérent. Compter environ une heure et demie.

Pour la présentation, pensez toujours à respecter une marge, le correcteur vous en saura gré.

I. Production semi-guidée (100 à 150 mots).

Le sujet a souvent un lien direct avec le texte de la partie compréhension (imaginer un dialogue entre les personnages après la scène, etc.). Le niveau de langue est en général celui de la conversation courante, d'autant que l'on demande fréquemment de rédiger un dialogue, le plus souvent polémique. Le sujet vous fixe des consignes grammaticales (par exemple utiliser des modaux) ou notionnelles-fonctionnelles (exprimer le regret, l'admiration, la colère, la comparaison...). Dans ce dernier cas, faire au brouillon **une liste** des expressions que l'on connaît pour exprimer telle ou telle notion-fonction et s'astreindre ensuite à en employer le plus grand nombre possible, puisque c'est là-dessus que l'on évaluera cette partie. On vous demande d'ailleurs souvent de souligner ces expressions.

II. Production libre (200 à 250 mots).

Vous avez deux sujets au choix, portant sur des questions de société contemporaine qui peuvent avoir (mais ce n'est pas nécessairement le cas) un lien avec le texte. On attend une pensée claire, une expression aisée et idiomatique. Dans le cas d'un sujet de réflexion, s'astreindre à employer les mots de liaison et les termes de l'argumentation logique. Pour le plan, une bonne méthode consiste à faire un canevas très succinct au brouillon, sur la colonne de gauche, tout en notant dans la colonne de droite les mots et expressions que l'on tient absolument à réemployer à telle ou telle étape.

Il est bien sûr vivement conseillé de s'entraîner en apprenant du vocabulaire portant sur des sujets de société (notamment avec *English in the News*), mais l'essentiel est sans doute d'être le plus souvent possible en contact avec de l'anglais authentique en contexte : presse, romans, nouvelles, films, tous les moyens sont bons pour accroître votre vocabulaire.

Soigner évidemment la présentation (une copie propre et lisible prédispose le correcteur en votre faveur) et toujours prendre le temps de se relire pour les fautes d'orthographe ou de grammaire (-s des terminaisons, etc.).

Bon travail !

LANGUE VIVANTE I

Barèmes

	A1-A3	A2	B
A. Compétence linguistique	30	25	35
B. Compréhension de l'écrit	35	35	35
C. Expression personnelle	35	40	30

SUJET

A. COMPÉTENCE LINGUISTIQUE

I. Pour former un nom à partir des verbes suivants, quel suffixe faut-il ?

al - ment - tion ou ∅

Donnez pour chaque verbe le nom correspondant.

1. renew: ....
2. reduce: ....
3. approve: ....
4. improve: ....
5. accuse: ....

6. refuse: ....
7. confine: ....
8. imagine: ....
9. exclaim: ....
10. claim: ....

II. Réécrivez les expressions suivantes en remplaçant les symboles ou abréviations et les nombres par le mot écrit en toutes lettres.

1. 3 m. people ....
2. A £2 ticket ....
3. 20 p. off ....

4. An M.P. ....
5. In the 30s ....
6. $\dfrac{2}{3}$ of the population ....

III. Mettez le verbe entre parenthèses au temps et à la forme voulus de la voix active ou de la voix passive.

A bomb (to blow up) .... at the Hilton Hotel yesterday morning while several Euro-ministers (to hold) ....
.... a conference in a building nearby. Fortunately, only a few people (to wound) .... since the staff (to expect) .....
.... it to happen for some time. Apparently, the hotel manager received repeated messages at the beginning of last month and (to think) .... it wiser to notify the police. He (to be) .... on his guard ever since. The investigation (to begin) .... but Inspector Smith (to refuse) ......
.... so far to make any further declaration. When the terrorists (to arrest) ...., the population, no doubt, (to relieve) ....

IV. For + infinitif ou gérondif?
Complétez avec l'infinitif ou le gérondif.

"Of course", said the Prime Minister, "the government can't be blamed for
.... (not/try) to do anything.

We took these measures for .... (every-body/know) what we've done so far.

It's very difficult for .... (us/enforce) these deci-sions. We apologize for .... (not/satisfy) every-body.

We thank everyone for .... (support/us) in our efforts."

V. A chaque phrase correspond une explication. Entourez la lettre pour chaque explication choisie.

1. I remember posting your letter. a) Je l'ai fait.
   b) C'est à faire.

2. I can't bear to see it. a) Chaque fois que je le vois je ressens la même chose.
   b) Je ne le regarderai donc pas.

3. He stopped to talk to his friend. a) Il s'est arrêté de parler.
   b) Il s'est arrêté pour parler.

4. I regret speaking to you about it. a) Je le regrette mais je le fais.
   b) Je le regrette mais je l'ai fait.

B. COMPRÉHENSION D'UN TEXTE ÉCRIT

DEIRDRE : I'm leaving, Ma. I'm getting out.

THERESA : (*Looking at her*) Getting out where to?

DEIRDRE : England.

THERESA : What are you talking about? You've got three wee children.

5 DEIRDRE : I'm taking them with me.

THERESA : (*Concerned*) Deirdre, love... (*Angry*) For crying out loud, will you sit down.

(*Pause.* DEIRDRE *does so.*)

What are you going to do in England, with three wee child-

10 ren?

DEIRDRE : I'm going, that's all. I have to get away. I can't take any more.

THERESA : Look, love, I know it isn't easy for you here, but... well, you've got friends here. You've got me and Joan here. Over

15 there you'll have nobody. Where will you live? What'll you do for money? You can't just go over there nowadays and live on the National Assistance.

DEIRDRE : We'll get something. They'll not let us starve.

THERESA : No, they'll probably send you straight back - especially when

20 they find out about him.

DEIRDRE : I'll use a false name. I'll think of something. I've got to get away, I've got to. Do you have any money? You've something in the post office... I'll pay you back... just to get me settled.

25 THERESA : Deirdre, for goodness sake, be practical. How could you get a job? Who would look after the kids when you were at work?

DEIRDRE : I could always pay a baby sitter.

THERESA : You couldn't afford to live over there, pay rent, feed and clothe you all, and pay a full-time babysitter.

30 DEIRDRE : I screamed this morning. I screamed and threw three cups against the wall.

THERESA : Where were the children?

DEIRDRE : Ducking. (*Pause*) It happens all the time up there - women screaming, for all sorts of reasons. That's what we mean by
35 the dawn chorus.

(THERESA *looks at her for a moment.*)

THERESA : You're not running off with another man, are you?

DEIRDRE : Oh aye, isn't the country just full of men dying to look after another man's three kids? If I could get a man life might be
40 bearable.

THERESA : Why don't you try for a wee part-time job here? You could do home help or something.

DEIRDRE : Ma, I want away from here.

THERESA : Well, I just don't see how you're going to manage.

45 DEIRDRE : You could help me.

THERESA : Deirdre, I don't think the little money I have in the post office would help you very much at all. [...]

DEIRDRE : You don't realize how serious this is. You don't know how badly I need to get away. I'm going mad. I'm just screaming
50 inside. I'm sometimes afraid I'm going to do something to me, or one of the kids.

THERESA : You'll have to tell Joe. You can't just walk out on him, without any warning.

DEIRDRE : Do you know what would happen if I told him? He'd set his
55 mates on me. I wouldn't be allowed to go anywhere. Why should I have to suffer for what he did? [...]

THERESA : Suppose there's an amnesty?

DEIRDRE : I'll cut my throat. (*Pause*). Do you think what Joe did was wrong?

60 THERESA : Of course I think it was wrong. I think the people who murdered our Peter were wrong. He was innocent. At least the ones Joe shot were involved.

DEIRDRE : (*Looking at her*) They were like our Peter, Ma. They were somebody's sons... somebody's brothers... one of them was
65 somebody's husband and the father of three children.

(*Pause*). How will I bring up my children, Ma? What will I tell them? Your Uncle Peter was killed by murderers - but your dad's a hero for murdering others?

11

THERESA : They'll have to make up their own minds when they're old
70   enough.
DEIRDRE : Ma, we live in Northern Ireland. My children won't have their
       own minds when they're old enough.
       (*Pause. They glance at each other. Silence.*)
       I've never asked you for anything, never. Please, Ma, will you
75   help me now ?

                   Graham Reid, *Remembrance* II, 14. (1985).

1. Find two elements, of a different nature (quotations, typography, etc.),
   which enable us to realize that this text is an excerpt from a play.
   . . . .

2. The text opposes "here" to "there". Give the name of those places
   "there": . . . .
   "here": . . . .

3. What do "they" and "him" in the text refer to ?
   Friends   "The people who murdered our Peter"
   Joe and Uncle Peter   British immigration officials
   British social services   "The ones Joe shot"
   Joe
   a) "THEY"
   Write down the correct answers:

they (1.18)	they & they (1.19)	they & they (1.63)

   b) "HIM": 1.20:

4. Deirdre:
   a) What is most vital for Deirdre ? (Tick the right answer)
      a) immigrating into a specific country.
      b) emigrating from the place where she lives.
         Pick out the two adverbial particles which justify your choice (1.1
         to 1.14)
         . . . .
   b) Deirdre sometimes reacts violenty. Find in the text three sentences in
      which she either acts violently or threatens to do so.
      . . . .
      . . . .
      . . . .
   c) Does it mean that she doesn't care about her children ?
      ☐ yes   ☐ no
      Justify by quoting from the text.
      . . . .

5. Deirdre and Theresa.
   a) (*Pause.* DEIRDRE *does so.*) (1.8)
      What does "does so" refer to ? . . . .

b) Find 2 sentences which prove that Deirdre is sarcastic.

....

....

c) For Theresa, there are two categories of victims:
   those who where killed although they were ....

   and those who were killed because they were ....
   (complete each sentence with one word from the text)
   True or False, tick the right box and justify. (1.16 to the end)

	T	F
d) Deirdre objects to her mother's view.	☐	☐

....

| e) Deirdre is pessimistic; she knows that the future generations will perpetuate the conflict in her country. | ☐ | ☐ |

....

| f) Deirdre has always relied on her mother for help. | ☐ | ☐ |

....

| g) Joe has no way of preventing Deirdre from leaving. | ☐ | ☐ |

....

6. Translate from English into French.
   1.26. Who would look after the kids when you were at work?

....

   1.52-53. You'll have to tell Joe. You can't just walk out on him without any warning.

....

....

C. EXPRESSION PERSONNELLE

I. Production semi-guidée (100 à 150 mots).

   Deirdre writes to Theresa from England and describes the <u>difficulties</u> she has to face. She expresses her <u>worries</u> and her <u>fears</u>, but finishes on a <u>hopeful</u> note.

II. Production libre (200 à 250 mots).

Traitez l'un des deux sujets au choix.

1. An American survey in 1990 showed that the under 30 generation is less interested in the news. What, in the American context, can account for their attitude?

2. Would you agree to work abroad if you were asked to do so? Say why or why not, going through the advantages and drawbacks of such a situation.

CORRIGÉS

49,5 → reduire sur 40 (×2)

A. COMPÉTENCE LINGUISTIQUE

I (17,5)

1. renewal *0,5*
2. reduction
3. approval
4. improvement
5. accusation

6. refusal
7. confinement
8. imagination
9. exclamation
10. claim

II

1. three million people *0, 5*
2. a two-pound ticket
3. twenty pence off

4. a Member of Parliament
5. in the thirties
6. two thirds of the population

III

blew up - were holding - were wounded - had been expecting - (had) thought - had been - has begun - has refused - are arrested - will be relieved.

IV

not trying - everybody to know - us to enforce - not satisfying - supporting us.

V

1a; 2b; 3b; 4a.

(16)

B. COMPRÉHENSION D'UN TEXTE ÉCRIT

1. The speakers (Deirdre and Theresa) are named at the beginning of *0,5* their lines.
   The title of the book includes act and scene references (*Remembrance* II, 14).
   The text includes stage directions (e.g. "looking at her", 1.2).

2. *There* = England *0, 5*   *Here* = Northern Ireland.

wee children e l(4) Tout petits

3.
a) They (1.18) = British social services.
They and they (1.19) = British immigration officials.
They and they (1.63) = the ones Joe shot.
b) Him (1.20) = Joe.

4.
b) emigrating from the place where she lives.
"I'm getting out" (1.1).
"I have to get away" (1.11).
b) "I screamed and threw three cups against the wall" (1.30).
– "[…] I'm going to do something to me, or one of the kids"
(1.50).
– "I'll cut my throat" (1.58). *I'm screaming inside (1.69)*
c) No.
"I'm sometimes afraid I'm going to do something to me, or
one of the kids." *I'm taking them with me (15)*
"How will I bring up my children, Ma?" *I could always pay a baby-sitter*

5.
a) does so = sits down. *2 (71.72 My children*
b) That's what we mean by the dawn chorus. (1.34) *won't have their*
isn't the country just full of men dying to look after another *own mind"*
man's three kids? (1.38-39)
c) Those who were killed although they were *innocent* and those
who were killed because they were *involved.* *→ I've got to go away*
d) True. "They were like our Peter, ma" (1.63). *(48→69 You don't)*
e) True. "My chidren won't have their own minds when they are *always*
old enough" (1.69).
f) False. "I've never asked you for anything" (1.74).
g) False. "He'd set his mates on me" (1.54). "I wouldn't be
allowed to go anywhere" (1.55).

6.
a) Qui s'occuperait des enfants quand tu serais au travail?
b) Il faudra bien que tu en parles à Joe. Tu ne peux (Tu ne vas) tout
de même pas le plaquer sans le prévenir.

Uncle Peter was killed.
Joe = Deirdre's husband killed
some people

C. EXPRESSION PERSONNELLE

I. Expression semi-guidée

Dear Mum
I'm sorry I haven't written in ages, but things have been quite difficult over here. I lost that job in the pub I'd told you about, they didn't

15

extend my contract at the end of the trial period - as if you needed any special skills to serve drinks. They wouldn't even let me stay on as a cleaning lady because they'd already got one - an Englishwoman of course. I've been down to a couple of job centres but none of them seems to be offering positions at the moment, or if they do I haven't got the right qualifications. I also got worried about Seamus because his stomach had been playing up for the last couple of weeks, I can't help feeling he misses his friends from school. Thank God Moraig seems to be adjusting all right. She's even made a new friend whose father is looking for a secretary, I'm meeting him at his office tomorrow so things might work out after all. I hope you're OK, don't worry about me. Love.

Deirdre.

II. Expression libre

1. Young Americans nowadays are reported to have a diminishing interest in the news: they don't read the papers or watch the news much, which might account for the low rate of active voters in the States today. Indeed, in order to reverse this process, some politicized rap bands have gone so far as to insist that concert goers should prove they were registered voters to get admission to their gigs. Something is definitely wrong with American democracy and public awareness in general. However, rather than assume a self-righteous stance, we might as well ask ourselves how this sorry state of affairs came into being. Part of it may be a backlash from the sixties and the seventies: after those heady decades of political activism, many young people got disenchanted with politics and started focusing on private issues again, earning themselves the 'me-generation' nickname. On the other hand, the current lack of public awareness among the under-thirties in America might be due to the rampant development of mass entertainment: who wants to watch some depressing news report when you can just as easily plug into MTV and bang your head to the latest heavy metal band? Far from being a joke, this hints at a more serious argument: young people in a post-industrial society can no longer identify with broad political issues because they feel too helpless; if anything, they'd rather start a garage band with a couple of friends. However, this might ultimately lead to a renewal of interest in public issues, starting from a private perspective rather than some holier-than-thou principles; not such a bad thing, at the end of the day.

2. If I were offered to work abroad, I think I would grab that opportunity for fear it might not happen again; so if I ever got promoted to a foreign position without any say in the matter (which incidentally is becoming increasingly common, what with international companies and the EEC), I wouldn't feel sorry for myself for a minute; quite the opposite, I think I'd start packing immediately! Indeed, I know as a fact that travelling stretches your imagination and your understanding of other people, so working abroad for any length of time would be an irreplaceable opportunity to discover new values and a new lifestyle - not to mention learning a new language. Besides, I would probably get expatriation allowance, which would make the stay quite rewarding financially: indeed, many people who've had an experience of working abroad never want to go back to their country of origin once they've had a taste of something else. However, I don't underestimate the drawbacks of expatriation: even if the company you work for pays for your spouse and your children to be relocated along with you, you will still leave behind some friends and relatives whom you're bound to miss at some point. It then becomes a matter of how far from home you are: there is a world of difference between moving to Spain and moving to New Zealand! If you get homesick in Madrid, you can afford to hop on the first homebound plane; it becomes quite a different matter if you're dozens of thousands of kilometers from home. Having said all this, I'd love to have an opportunity to work and live abroad.

SUJET

A. COMPÉTENCE LINGUISTIQUE

I. Complétez les phrases en utilisant les articles the, a ou an. Utilisez le symbole ∅ si l'article n'est pas nécessaire.

Peter, 49, is five years younger than George. Their parents died when ......
(1) brothers were children, and Peter was brought up by ...... (2) uncle in
Newsbury. He joined ...... (3) Newsbury branch of merchant bank
Kleinwort Benson in 1960 - ...... (4) same year George joined ...... (5)
Metropolitan Police.
While George was doing everything from dealing with ...... (6) Iranian
embassy siege in 1981 to solving ...... (7) murder of seven Chinese people
in ...... (8) club in Soho, Peter was quietly making his way through ......
(9) back offices of Kleinwort. He landed in ...... (10) City in 1969 and
eventually became ...... (11) group's company secretary, when his prede-
cessor moved on to be ...... (12) Queen's press spokesman.

II. L'action exprimée par le verbe souligné a-t-elle été effectivement réalisée ou non? Cochez la case correspondant à votre réponse.

	OUI	NON
1. I was an odd child but I could <u>make</u> the class laugh, which is a great strength.		
2. I thought they might all like to <u>come</u> to supper at our house.		
3. I wish I <u>had</u> a place like this. Lots of things you can do in a place like this!		
4. Tell him we can <u>come</u> if we find a sitter.		
5. The chauffeur-driven car would <u>pick</u> her up from home every morning.		

III. *Complétez les éléments de la colonne 1 avec les éléments pris dans la colonne 2 pour que la conversation soit cohérente. Copiez les phrases sur les lignes laissées à cet effet.*

1	2
"Hi, Bernard, I'm Tom Wingo"	- he said, glancing at me briefly
....	- he said in a hostile voice
"Yeah, I thought it was you"	- I said, extending my hand
....	- I shouted to warn him of my approach
"How are you doing?"	- he answered
....	- I admitted
"I'm okay"	- he said when I neared him
....	- I asked
"Been waiting long here?"	
....	
"Long enough"	
....	
"I got lost, I always get lost in Central Park"	
....	
"No one asked you to come here"	
....	

IV. *Combinez les éléments pris dans les colonnes 1 et 2 de manière à obtenir des phrases cohérentes : ajoutez les mots de liaison qui conviennent.*

1	2
1. Nobody came to that part of the country...	a. her extreme youth.
2. Sometimes he spoke out loud to himself...	b. they had told him they were free.
3. She was not shy...	c. he wouldn't have completed his work.
4. She was no taller than him...	d. they were obliged to.
5. He had to work longer hours...	e. driving his lorry.
6. They couldn't refuse his invitation...	f. much older.

V. *Complétez les phrases en mettant le verbe entre parenthèses au temps et à la forme qui conviennent.*

1. He .... (to stand) on the porch in darkness, staring at us through the glass-panelled door. I did not know how long he .... (to watch) us.

2. Now 73, she . . . . (to write) more than 40 books.

3. The country . . . . (to be) months without rain: the people are starving.

4. She regularly . . . . (to call) friends for news, now she's living in London.

5. "Tom", she whispered "if I ask you something seriously, ... (you answer) me?"

6. I will have to point out how different things are now. But then Miss Kenton is an intelligent woman and she . . . . (already realize) these things.

7. I won't pay the builder until he . . . . (to finish) his work.

8. To my surprise, once we . . . . (to finish) interviewing the girl, my partner suggested we . . . . (to hire) her.

B. COMPRÉHENSION D'UN TEXTE ÉCRIT

Okay, picture this: a table, dinner, my parents, my teenage brother, me (dressed in a sari so that I look like a very nice Indian girl), and... IT!

IT talks about himself, his career, his family, his brilliant ideas on the political situation in India, his speculations on racism in Britain today...
5 My father nods, my mother smiles in admiration, my brother is bored out of his mind. And I continue to pretend that I am a very nice Indian girl, for IT is really a very nice Indian boy, and this is the mise-en-scène of a modern arranged marriage.

Gone are the days when the boy, his father, the boy's grandfather, the
10 boy's paternal uncles and the boy's best friend would dress up and arrive at the home of the prospective bride. The girl would sit with her father and look as sweet as she could (because her looks were the most crucial factor) and she would not speak unless spoken to. She may have been asked to sing for the men; perhaps she would have prepared some
15 sweetmeats[1] for them to eat. This was how my mother was introduced to the world of marriage. She was so nervous that she did not even look at the prospective groom. Mummy did not know what daddy looked like until the wedding day.

Nowadays, far away from the motherland, arranged marriage is not so
20 humiliating for the girl. As well as unofficial match-making (a much favoured pastime of Indian housewives) we have marriage columns in Indian newspapers. A typical ad: Alliance for tall (1.78m), fair Brahim doctor aged 28. Beautiful, slim, highly educated traditional girl wanted.

(...) I learnt a long time ago to take it all with a pinch of salt[2]. It is
25 humiliating to be told to dress up and look pretty and act like a highly educated, docile girl all evening. But it is not the end of the world. Yes, I

---

1. sweetmeats: *sucreries.*
2. to take with a pinch of salt: not to take too seriously.

want to get married. Yes, I want to marry someone my parents will approve of. Yes, I have met all the prospective grooms they have found for me. And yes, I have not liked a single one of them.

30   They are all ITs to me and since under my sari I am a wicked girl, I generally give them a hard time.

Dirty looks are an efficient ploy. Or fits of wheezing[3] at the dinner table to make an IT think I have some strange ailment; my brother might join in this one - we can wheez in sync[4] - to make it look hereditary. I

35   might try the sultry technique designed to turn an IT into a nervous twit[5]. I'll start pouting my lips and batting my eyelids and heaving my chest. If IT should survive these tricks there is always the Spanish Inquisition Method. I have compiled a set of questions that even the Gestapo would have been too polite to ask. My parents are used by now

40   to seeing a perfectly confident young man walk into the house and, after dinner, see him walk out a total wreck.

We have never called an IT back.

Indrani Nag-Chaudhury
in the Independent on Sunday, 23 June 1991 (abridged).

- **Compréhension globale**

I. This article was published in a Sunday newspaper. In which section would you have found it? (tick the right answer.)

a) Foreign affairs
b) Food and drink
c) Real Life
d) Going out.

II. The narrator is   a) a journalist
                   b) an Indian girl living in England
                   c) an Indian girl living in India.

Justify: (2 quotes)
1. . . . . Line . . . .
2. . . . . Line . . . .

III. The tone of the article is   a)   pathetic
                                   b)   serious
                                   c)   light
                                   d)   satirical.

IV. In your opinion which headline would best suit the article?

a) ARRANGED MARRIAGES: AN OUTMODED CUSTOM
b) ARRANGED MARRIAGES... AND HOW TO AVOID THEM
c) INDIAN GIRL DEFIES PARENTS OVER MARRIAGE

---

3. wheezing: as when suffering from asthma.
4. sync: synchronization.
5. twit: idiot.

Justify: (2 quotes)

1... Line........
2... Line........

- **Compréhension détaillée**

I. Find the equivalents of the following words or expressions in the text:

1. a traditional dress worn by Hindu women: ....
2. to bow one's head in sign of agreement: ....
3. arranging marriages: ....
4. a would-be husband: ....
5. naughty: ....
6. a trick: ....
7. seductive: ....
8. a ruin: ....

II. Right or wrong? Justify by quoting from the text.

1. Indrani enjoys dressing up and looking pretty.   R - W
.... Line........
2. She's not as sweet as she looks.   R - W
.... Line........
3. Her parents seem to appreciate the young man's conversation.   R - W
.... Line........
4. Her brother sides with her.   R - W
.... Line........
5. She's got a hereditary disease.   R - W
.... Line........
6. She has been faced with the same situation several times
   already.   R - W
.... Line........
7. The young men usually enjoy the time they spend with her.   R - W
.... Line........
8. Indrani's parents ask them to fill in a questionnaire.   R - W
.... Line........

III. Does she call the prospective grooms IT because...

a) she isn't told their names?
b) she despises them?
c) they mean nothing to her?

Justify: (2 quotes)

1... Line........
2... Line........

IV. Quote 2 of the tricks she likes to play on the young men.

1.. Line........
2.. Line........

V. Circle the adjectives which might be used to describe Indrani's ambiva-
lent attitude to modern arranged marriages:

BITTER / IRREVERENT / DOCILE / CONCILIATORY / REVOLUTION-
ARY

VI. a) Pick out 4 sentences in the text to show what was expected from the
girl when Indrani's mother "was introduced to the world of marriage":

1.. Line........
2.. Line........
3.. Line........
4.. Line........

b) What has changed according to Indrani? Quote from the text:

1.. Line........

VII. Translate from **If IT should survive** *(l. 37) to* **a total wreck** *(l. 41).*

C. EXPRESSION PERSONNELLE

I. Production semi-guidée (150 mots environ).

Indrani, the young Indian girl, eventually falls in love with... a *white* man.
She doesn't want to hurt her parents' feelings and asks an agony aunt* for
advice. Write the answer to her letter as it was published in the magazine.
Use MODALS, expressions of ADVICE, SUGGESTION.

II. Production libre (250 mots environ).

Au choix:
1. Tradition and modernity: can we reconcile the one with the other?
Give precise examples.

2. The U.S.A. was once considered the land of the "melting pot". Is this still
true in the 1990's? Is total integration the solution to the problems of immigration or should each community's identity be preserved?

---

* personne responsable du courrier du cœur dans un magazine.

CORRIGÉS

A. COMPÉTENCE LINGUISTIQUE

I

1. the	7. the
2. an	8. a
3. the	9. the
4. the	10. the
5. the	11. the
6. the	12. the

II

1. oui. 2. oui. 3. non. 4. non. 5. oui.

III

"Hi, Bernard, I'm Tom Wingo," *I shouted to warn him of my approach.*
"Yeah, I thought it was you," *he said, glancing at me briefly.*
"How are you doing?" *I said, extending my hand.*
"I'm okay," *he said when I neared him.*
"Been waiting here long?" *I asked.*
"Long enough," *he answered.*
"I got lost, I always get lost in Central Park", *I admitted.*
"No one asked you to come here", *he said in a hostile voice.*

IV

1. Nobody came to that part of the country unless they were obliged to.
2. Sometimes he spoke out loud to himself while driving his lorry.
3. She was not shy in spite of her extreme youth.
4. She was no taller than him though much older.
5. He had to work longer hours, otherwise he wouldn't have completed his work.
6. They couldn't refuse his invitation because they had told him they were free.

V

1. was standing; had been watching.
2. has written.
3. has been.
4. calls.
5. will you answer.
6. has already realized.
7. finishes.
8. had finished; (should) hire.

B. COMPRÉHENSION D'UN TEXTE ÉCRIT

• Compréhension globale

I

c) Real Life.

II

b) an Indian girl living in England.
1. "me (dressed in a sari like a nice Indian girl)", l.2
2. "Nowadays, far away from the motherland", l.19

III

d) satirical

IV

ARRANGED MARRIAGES... AND HOW TO AVOID THEM
1. "But it is not the end of the world", l.26
2. "I generally give them (= ITs = prospective bridegrooms) a hard time", l.31

• Compréhension détaillée

I

1. a sari	5. wicked
2. to nod	6. a ploy
3. matchmaking	7. sultry
4. a prospective groom	8. a wreck

II

1. WRONG
"It is humiliating to be told to […]", l.24.
2. RIGHT
"under my sari I am a wicked girl", l.30.
3. RIGHT
"My father nods, my mother smiles in admiration", l.5.
4. RIGHT
"My brother might join in this one", l.33
5. WRONG
"to make it <u>look</u> hereditary", l.34.
6. RIGHT
"I have met all the prospective grooms they have found for me",
l.28.
7. WRONG
"see him walk out a total wreck", l.41.
8. WRONG
"<u>I</u> have compiled <u>a set of questions</u>", l.38.

III

c) They mean nothing to her.
"for IT is really a very nice Indian boy", l.7.
"I have not liked a single one of them", l.29.

IV

1. "dirty looks"
2. "pouting my lips and batting my eyelids and heaving my chest".
3. "fits of wheezing".
4. "a set of questions that even the Gestapo would have been too polite
to ask ".

V

IRREVERENT/CONCILIATORY

VI

a) 1. "She would look as sweet as she could", l.12.
   2. "She would not speak unless spoken to", l.13.
   3. "She may have been asked to sing for the men".
   4. "Perhaps she would have prepared some sweetmeats for them to
      eat", l.14
b) "Nowadays, […] arranged marriage is not so humiliating for the
   girl", l.19.

VII

Si par malheur il arrive à survivre à tous ces mauvais tours, il reste toujours la Technique de l'Inquisition espagnole. J'ai mis au point une série de questions que la Gestapo elle-même n'aurait pas eu l'indélicatesse de poser. Mes parents ont désormais l'habitude de voir arriver les jeunes gens en pleine possession de leurs moyens, et ressortir après le dîner à l'état de véritables loques.

C. EXPRESSION ÉCRITE

I. Expression semi-guidée

Dear Indrani,

You should not let feelings of guilt prevent you from loving whoever you may love. The young man you mentioned in your letter seems perfectly nice so I can see no reason for you to stop seeing him. However, as you are aware, your parents may react negatively when you first introduce your boyfriend to them. Why not discuss this with him beforehand? You might even want to rehearse the conversation with your parents together if he is willing to do so. Then how about mentioning your boyfriend to your brothers and sisters, or to an aunt or uncle who might give you some advice on how to handle your parents? This is by no means an easy situation to cope with but remember, your parents love you and eventually, they can only approve of your happiness.

II. Expression libre

1. In many respects, the modern era is torn between tradition and modernity. This is true with regard to private morality as well as in more general matters of lifestyle and aesthetics. Should you get married or just live together "in sin ", as people used to say? Should you furnish your home with the latest designer furniture or be happy to live among ancient heirlooms? Should you buy all the latest hits or just keep playing your older brother's collection of Pink Floyd on vinyl? Many people answer these questions instinctively, which only goes to show that the split between tradition and modernity may not be as radical as it seems. Indeed, most of us develop a kind of Levi-Straussian *bricolage* in order to deal with the contradictions of a culture in motion. For example, many couples who are merely "living together" will be as genuinely devoted to each other as if they were actually married; you may blend different styles of furniture from the most quaint to the most radically hip; you may also enjoy various kinds of music for different occasions: techno or hip hop at parties, and string quartets when you are on your own! Indeed, it feels as if we were moving beyond the call for the all-modern, and learning to enjoy different styles and values in different contexts. Maybe this is what genuine modernity is all about, as opposed to the superficial, aggressive modern*ism* which held sway until the mid-seventies: we can now sit back and enjoy the rewards of a living culture, fondly but not over-reverently aware of its own past.

2. The U.S.A., once described as a "melting-pot", is rapidly turning into something akin to a tossed salad. Whereas nineteenth-century European immigrants blended quite successfully into a relatively harmonious mixture under the aegis of the original English-speaking settlers, postwar immigration shows signs of a growing splintering of the American social scene. U.S. Hispanics, for example, are notorious for their ability to develop their own social and economic networks, so much so that you can live quite happily in New York City without speaking a word of English these days. Asian Americans, while focusing on the West Coast, have also managed to retain many idiosyncratic cultural features. Finally, Black Americans now call themselves Afro Americans in an attempt to recapture their cultural identity at the expense of integration into WASP America. Many feel concerned by this trend towards cultural and ethnic fragmentation, inasmuch as it threatens the hegemony of English-speaking, Eurocentric culture in the States. But are there any easy solutions? It seems impractical, if not downright impossible, to force minorities determined to retain their specificity into a unifying mould. Maybe the time has come to recognize that America consists of many groups with different cultural backgrounds, a fact which schooling and public facilities might want to take into account. Bilingual schooling, official forms and road signs are a few examples that spring to mind. Would the U.S.A. be any the worse for it? Each community may now need some special recognition in order to live in harmony with one another.

SUJET

A. COMPÉTENCE LINGUISTIQUE

I. Fill the blanks in the following passage. Use only ONE word in each space. (A short form such as **didn't, can't,** or **won't is** considered as one word.)

Brenda Linson never . . . . (1) anywhere without an empty spectacles case. It is . . . . (2) vital to her as her purse. Yet, she doesn't wear glasses. The reason she can't do without it is because she can neither read . . . . (3) write. If . . . . (4) she gets into any situation where she might . . . . (5) expected to do either of these things, she fishes around in her bag for the specs case, finds it's empty, and asks the person concerned to . . . . (6) the reading for her.

Brenda is now in her late thirties, and until a few months . . . . (7) hardly . . . . (8) knew she was illiterate. Her husband didn't know and her children didn't know. The children still . . . . (9). It . . . . (10) never occurred to them that their . . . . (11) cannot read... She doesn't . . . . (12) them stories, but their father doesn't either, ... (13) they find nothing surprising in this fact.

She has . . . . (14) number of tactics for concealing her difficulty . . . . (15) example, never lingering near a phone at work, in case she has to answer it and might be . . . . (16) to write something . . . . (17). In fact, it is easier . . . . (18) illiterates to conceal the truth . . . . (19) one might . . . . (20).

Adapted from *The Observer*, May 25, 1975.

II. Fill each of the blanks with a word formed from the word given in capital letters.

Example: He went upstairs so . . . .
. . . . that he woke the baby.   NOISE
→ He went upstairs so noisily that he woke the
baby.

1. His employer blamed him for being so . . . .
. . . .   RESPONSIBLE

2. The Times is a very famous . . . .
. . . . newspaper.   DAY

3. You never know how he's going to react, he's so
. . . .   PREDICT

4. Unfortunately, lots of school-leavers are hit by
. . . .   EMPLOY

5/6. . . . . and . . . .
. . . . are major social problems.   HOME/POOR

7. Travelling is said to . . . .
the mind.   BROAD

8. He has a fairly good . . . .
of German history.   KNOW

9/10. Although I like him I sometimes . . . .
. . . . of his . . . .   APPROVE/BEHAVE

III. In the following series of three words, circle the one which does not rhyme with the two other.

1. *bare*   -   *bear*   -   *beer*
2. *cheat* -   *sweat* -   *threat*
3. *blood* -   *flood* -   *wood*
4. *boot*   -   *foot*   -   *moon*
5. *root*   -   *route* -   *shout*

IV. Translate the following sentences

1. Souhaiteriez-vous une tasse de thé ?
. . . .

2. Depuis combien de temps êtes-vous ici ?
. . . .

3. Êtes-vous déjà allé en Italie ?
. . . .

4. Combien de fois le voyez-vous par mois ?
. . . .

5. Je n'ai aucune intention d'aller lui rendre visite.
. . . .

V. Rewrite the following sentences using the prompts below.

1. You can go out provided you promise to be back before midnight.
   → You can't go out . . . .
2. She seems to be used to speaking in public.
   → It's certainly not the first time . . . .
3. I sent for the doctor because I wanted him to examine the baby.
   → I sent for the doctor in order to . . . .
4. I can't help being nervous when I travel.
   → Travelling . . . .
5. In spite of her absence we had great fun.
   → Although . . . .

B. COMPRÉHENSION D'UN TEXTE ÉCRIT

     East Bradley Junior was just about the smallest school in Somerset; threats of closure rumbled like thunder round its ears, and perhaps it was the noise of that thunder which deafened Mr Rossiter, the Headmaster, to the murmured protests of children and staff as he stalked the corri-
5 dors, snapping at the children (and usually the wrong children), demanding peace, quiet and order in classrooms, school hall, staff room, everywhere, putting pupils in corners for wearing red socks, disallowing trainers, and even standing infant wrongdoers in the wastepaper basket to prove just how worthless their chatter was. The two dinner ladies had
10 caught his manner. Children who did not eat up were made to eat up, which kept Mrs Windsor busy cleaning up pupils who had been unexpectedly and distressingly sick. Mr Rossiter hated the PTA[1], but had to have one. The PTA raised money and the school was short of money. Without the parents, the school secretary would have had no typewriter,
15 let alone paper for the endless notes, messages and reproaches which streamed out of the school to the parental world. Mr Rossiter had liked the old days, when a line had been painted on the school playground and a notice above it said. 'No Parents Beyond This Point'; even though the LEA's[2] policy had obliged him to remove these in the mid-sixties, it
20 was the mid-seventies before the parents had ventured over the nonexistent line. But now there seemed no keeping them out. The new-style parents – mostly the ones down from London – would be in the classrooms before school, after school, chatting to teachers and pupils, even popping their heads round doors while lessons were in progress, with
25 messages about aunties or swimsuits or lost packed lunches. Lots of pupils took packed lunches. Mr Rossiter didn't like that. It somehow loosened the school's grip upon the child. It smacked of change: change smacked of chaos.

---

1. PTA: Parent-teachers-associations.
2. LEA: Local Education Authority.

The names on the school register[3] changed as the community outside
30   changed. The ordinary Alans and Lindas and Michaels and Annes were
sprinkled with[4] Saffrons and Ishtars, Sebs and Felixes. The old stone
villages were infilled with bungalows and housing estates.
   And the parents seemed to divide these days into the rich and the poor.
New Volvos drove up to the school gates while from the school bus
35   limped children who were wearing someone else's shoes, because the
parents couldn't afford new.

Adapted from Kay WELDON'S *JUST WOMEN*, 1989.

● **Compréhension globale**

1. <u>*Choose the most appropriate title for this passage.*</u> *(Circle the right ans-*
wer.)
   a) Threats of closure on the school.
   b) The ideal Junior High School.
   c) The world is changing. So is East Bradley Junior.
   d) Yes, I hate school!

2. <u>*The place presented is located in*</u> *(Circle the right answer.)*
   a) Scotland.
   b) England.
   c) Wales.
   d) Ireland.

3. <u>*The main character's name is*</u> *(Circle the right answer.)*
   a) Mr Rossiter.
   b) Mr Bradley.
   c) Mrs Windsor.

4. <u>*Choose two adjectives which correspond to the headmaster's character.*</u>
(Circle the right answer.)
   a) helpful.
   b) authoritarian.
   c) nostalgic.
   d) unconcerned.
   e) competent.

● **Compréhension approfondie**

I. Are these statement <u>true</u> or <u>false</u>? Quote from the text to justify your
answers. Indicate the lines.

   1. The school had no financial problems.
   . . . .
   . . . .
   2. The dinner ladies did not oblige the children to eat what they didn't like.
   . . . .
   . . . .

_____
3. school register: list of pupils of the school.   4. sprinkled with: mixed with.

3. Some pupils were ill after eating in the school canteen.

    . . . .
    . . . .

4. The headmaster didn't like the parents to interfere in school life.

    . . . .
    . . . .

5. The headmaster needed the parents.

    . . . .
    . . . .

6. It was exceptional to see parents in the school.

    . . . .
    . . . .

7. The villages near the school had not been affected by change.

    . . . .
    . . . .

8. New-style parents showed no interest in school life.

    . . . .
    . . . .

9. The headmaster wasn't new to the school.

    . . . .
    . . . .

10. The pupils families all belonged to the same social class.

    . . . .
    . . . .

II. Find the equivalents for these expressions (tick the right answer):

1. putting pupils in corners for wearing red socks (line 7) means:
    a) punishing pupils because they were wearing red socks.
    b) forcing pupils to wear red socks.
    c) telling pupils to leave their red socks in a corner.

2. It ... loosened the school's grip upon the child (line 26) means:
    a) The school lost more pupils every year.
    b) The children often got lost in the corridors of the school.
    c) The school was losing its authority over the children.

3. It smacked of change (line 27) means:
    a) It was time for a change.
    b) It was not time for a change.
    c) Things were going to change.

4. Change smacked of chaos (line 27) means:
    a) Mr Rossiter believed change would be a disaster for the school.
    b) New parents were really a nuisance.
    c) Strict discipline was necessary in this school.

III. The following statements concern Mr Rossiter, the headmaster. Find between line 1 and line 10 the word or phrase which shows that:

1. He was unreceptive to the problems of pupils and teachers.
   . . . .
2. He walked about the school in an authoritarian manner.
   . . . .
3. He didn't speak to the children in a pleasant manner.
   . . . .
4. He punished children in a most humiliating way simply for talking.
   . . . .
5. He was not the only person in the school to be unkind to the pupils.
   . . . .

IV. Translate the text from "The new-style parents" (l. 21) down to "smacked of chaos" (l. 28)

C. PRODUCTION ÉCRITE

I. Production semi-guidée.

Julie is a 13 year-old pupil at East Bradley Junior. She is now writing to her grandmother and complaining about life at school. She criticizes the strict rules and the attitudes of the headmaster and the dinner ladies. Write Julie's letter. (About 150 words.)

II. Production libre.

Traiter l'un de ces deux sujets au choix :
1. What is more important in the life of a teenager: the influence of his parents or the influence of school (teachers, friends, what one learns at school, etc.)? (About 250 words.)
2. Changes: are you afraid of them or do you consider that they make life more interesting? (About 250 words.)

CORRIGES

A. COMPÉTENCE LINGUISTIQUE

I

1. goes	8. anybody	15. For
2. as	9. don't	16. expected/asked
3. nor	10. has	17. down
4. ever	11. mother	18. for
5. be	12. read	19. than
6. do	13. so	20. think
7. ago	14. a	

II

1. irresponsible
2. daily
3. unpredictable
4. unemployment
5. Homelessness
6. poverty
7. broaden
8. knowlegde
9. disapprove
10. behaviour

III

1. beer
2. cheat
3. wood
4. foot
5. shout

IV

1. Would you like (Would you care for) a cup of tea?
2. How long have you been here?
3. Have you ever been to Italy?
4. How many times a month do you see him?
5. I have no intention of visiting her/him.

V

1. You can't go out *unless* you promise to be back before midnight.
2. It's certainly not the first time she has spoken (she speaks) in public.
3. I sent for the doctor in order to have the baby examined.
4. Travelling always makes me nervous.
5. Although she was absent (= away, not here), we had great fun.

B. COMPRÉHENSION D'UN TEXTE ÉCRIT

● **Compréhension globale**

1. c. 2. b. 3.a. 4. b; c.

• Compréhension approfondie

I

1. FALSE
"Threats of closure rumbled like thunder round its ears".
2. FALSE
"Children who did not eat up were made to eat up".
3. TRUE
"...cleaning up pupils who had been unexpectedly and distressingly sick".
4. TRUE
"No parents beyond this point".
5. FALSE
"Now there seemed no keeping them out".
6. FALSE
"The new-style parents [...] would be in the classrooms before school, after school ...".
7. FALSE
"The old stone villages were infilled with bungalows and housing estates".
8. FALSE
"...chatting to teachers and pupils, even popping their heads round doors while lessons were in progress".
9. TRUE
"...even though the LEA policy had obliged him to remove these in the mid-sixties, it was the mid-seventies before...".
10. FALSE
"And the parents seemed to divide these days between the rich and the poor".

II

1. a. 2. c. 3. c. 4. a.

III

1. "the murmured protests of children and staff".
2. "he stalked the corridors".
3. "snapping at the children".
4. "standing infant wrongdoers in the wastepaper basket to prove just how worthless their chatter was".
5. "The two dinner ladies had caught his manner".

IV

On trouvait des parents nouvelle formule (surtout ceux qui venaient de Londres) dans les salles de classe avant les cours, après les cours, en train de bavarder avec les professeurs et les élèves, voire en train de pointer le bout de leur nez en plein milieu d'un cours, avec des messages où il était question de Taties, de maillots de bain ou de casse-croûte égarés. Beaucoup d'élèves apportaient leur casse-croûte. Cela ne plaisait guère à Mr. Rossiter. Cela desserrait en quelque sorte l'emprise de l'école sur les élèves. Cela fleurait le changement; et le changement fleurait le chaos.

C. EXPRESSION PERSONNELLE

I. Expression semi-guidée

Dear Grannie,

How are you? I'm having a terrible time here: I keep getting into trouble for things I haven't done. Yesterday I was standing in the schoolyard and our headmaster accused me of making too much noise, he made me go and stand in a muddy corner for the whole time of the morning break. Then we're not supposed to loiter in the refectory after lunch; if we do, we have to stay in an extra hour after school to help clean the toilets. Ugh! Speaking of lunch, the dinner ladies are real cows: they bullied this ten year-old who wouldn't eat up his bread pudding (some disgusting soggy thing, they must have it specially delivered from a pet food shop), he was sick afterwards so they made him clean it all up. I do miss your homemade lemon cake. Do you think you could possibly send me some? Lots of love.

Julie

II. Expression libre

1. Not too many years ago, PTA's used to worry a lot about the respective influence of parents and school on the pliable minds of teenagers: what if some devious history teacher turned nice suburban youths into rampant fascists or lefties? Conversely, some teachers were all too ready to discuss the sorry influence of illiterate or narrow-minded parents on their offspring; finally, most parents used to worry and many still do, sometimes rightly so - about the unsavoury role - models their children are likely to encounter among their peers. Indeed, teenage is a phase during which most people stop looking up to their parents as the only reference available, which can result in family crises; however, many teenagers also go through their teens without any major clashes. After all, it is only fair to try to broaden your outlook, which needn't lead to a total rejection of the values you used to take for granted. In my opinion, a teenager's parents act as a kind of constant substratum with reference to which you try to define your own identity; in the process, you may start looking up to other adults such as teachers, but above all, you will identify with people in your own age-group. More often than not, this won't lead to anything more serious than a silly haircut or a funny taste in clothes, which most people eventually grow out of once they feel self-confident enough to assert themselves. Besides, we should not underestimate the positive aspects of this period of soul-searching: indeed, you may get to meet many interesting, worthwhile people who will have a beneficial influence over the rest of your life.

2. "Time may change me/But I can't trace time", as David Bowie used to sing. True, the most terrifying thing about the changes that affect you is that you can feel your grip on thing slipping without your even being aware of it: you suddenly look back on your past, or simply look around, and find a totally different landscape from the one you were accustomed to. You no longer have the same set of friends, your tastes have evolved, you have become a different person altogether. The funny thing is, you only become aware of those kinds of changes after the fact, as it were, once it's too late to do anything about them. This happened to me some time last year and I remember experiencing a bitter-sweet feeling, maybe because I realized for the first time what ageing was about, while welcoming what the future would bring. But there is also a different kind of change: apart from one's internal evolution, there are also external events which can seriously affect you, such as the death of a loved one or moving to a different city. I moved when I was ten, and even though it was only half a mile from my old house, I found it quite difficult to say goodbye to most of my elementary school friends. It made for a funny period of adjustment, which I was not entirely aware of at the time. But what about my friend from Martinique, who was uprooted at age twelve and only goes back home once every two years? This having been said, I'm not afraid of changes, no matter how painful they may be at first. After all, it's an ill wind that brings no good...

SUJET

A. COMPÉTENCE LINGUISTIQUE

I. A famous singer is being interviewed by a journalist. These are his answers. Try to find the questions.

1. . . . . ? - I have been singing for many years now.
2. . . . . ? - I think I'd rather play rock'n'roll than jazz.
3. . . . . ? - To the U.S.A. ? Two or three times a year.
4. . . . . ? - All these guitars are mine.
5. . . . . ? - I can't tell. A lot of money anyway.

II. LINK WORDS. Link the sentences using one of the following words. You may have to transform the sentences.

whenever / so that / in spite of / although / unless / whereas / whatever

1. The teacher was suspicious. The student had received no help at all for his essay.
2. The authorities sent five helicopters. All the families could be evacuated after the flood.
3. Someone should help me. I'll never be ready on time.
4. He often goes to London. He always brings back a present to his wife.
5. The pilot insisted on taking off. The weather conditions were very bad.

III. Turn the following sentences into the passive form.

1. They should call the fire brigade immediately.
2. They are building a new fast-food restaurant near our house.
3. The examination dates prevented her from going home early.

IV. Use the prompts to rewrite the sentences without changing the meaning.

1. I haven't seen him for three years.   • It's . . . .
2. What a pity I have to go now.   • I wish . . . .
3. One can't see anything.   • There's . . . . . .
4. Why are you complaining to the police about the noise your neighbours make ? You're wasting your time.   • It's . . . .
5. We've got to make a decision now.   • It's time . . . . .
6. It's not necessary to write such a letter.   • You . . . .
7. They certainly saw the burglar break into the house.   • They . . . .

V. Put the verbs between brackets in the correct tense and form.

Brain drain.

Some of China's best and brightest students [1] (can + find) these days in US university towns like Cambridge, Massachussetts and Berkeley, California. Since 1978, more than 170,000 Chinese students and scholars [2] (travel) abroad. Only a third of them [3] (return) to their home country so far. As a result, there is an acute shortage of scientists in China. Ninety per cent of Shanghai's senior scientists [4] (be) old enough to retire within the next decade.

Now, China [5] (promise) better pay to reverse this brain drain - a scientist currently [6] (earn) $37 a month, a laborer's wage. And last month, The Chinese government [7] (address) political dissidents in exile and [8] (welcome) them back.

Says Chen Kaili, a student in physics at the City University of New York: "I have no plan to return to China, even if there [9] (be) a position waiting for me because there can be no assurance that I [10] (be) allowed to leave the country again if I returned."

Adapted from "Time", Sept. 28, 1992.

VI. Justify your verb tense in 2, 4, 5, 7 and 10, quoting an indication given in the sentence.

B. COMPRÉHENSION D'UN TEXTE ÉCRIT

Whenever Henry Wilt took the dog for a walk, or, to be more accurate, when the dog took him, or, to be exact, when Mrs Wilt told them both to go and take themselves out of the house so that she could do her yoga exercices, he always took the same route. In fact the dog followed
5 the route and Wilt followed the dog. They went down past the Post Office, across the playground, under the railway bridge and out on to the footpath by the river. A mile along the river and then under the railway line again and back through streets where the houses were bigger than Wilt's semi[1] and where there were large trees and gardens and the cars
10 were all Rovers and Mercedes. It was here that Clem, a pedigree Labrador, evidently feeling more at home, did his business while Wilt

---

1. semi: semi-detached house..

stood looking around rather uneasily, conscious that this was not his sort of neighbourhood and wishing it was. It was about the only time during their walk that he was at all aware of his surroundings. For the rest of
15 the way Wilt's walk was an interior one. It was in fact a journey of wishful thinking[2], involving the irrevocable disappearance of Mrs Wilt, the sudden acquisition of wealth, power, what he would do if he was appointed Minister of Education or, better still, Prime Minister. It was partly concocted of a series of desperate expedients and partly in an uns-
20 poken dialogue so that anyone noticing Wilt (and most people didn't) might have seen his lips move occasionally and his mouth curl into what he fondly imagined was a sardonic smile as he dealt with questions or parried arguments with devastating repartee. It was on one of these walks taken in the rain after a particularly trying day at the Tech that
25 Wilt first conceived the notion that he would only be able to fulfil his latent promise and call his life his own if some not entirely fortuitous disaster overtook his wife.

Like everything else in Henry Wilt's life it was not a sudden decision. He was not a decisive man. Ten years as an Assistant Lecturer (Grade
30 Two) at the Fenland College of Arts and Technology was proof of that. For ten years he had remained in the Liberal Studies Department teaching classes of Gasfitters, Plasterers, Bricklayers and Plumbers. Or keeping them quiet.

To escape from the memory of Gasfitters as putative[3] human beings
35 and of Eva in the lotus position[4], Wilt walked by the river thinking dark thoughts, made darker still by the knowledge that for the fifth year running his application to be promoted to Senior Lecturer was almost certain to be turned down and that unless he did something soon he would be doomed to Gasfitters Three and Plasterers Two - and to Eva - for the rest
40 of his life. It was not a prospect to be borne. He would act decisively.

Tom SHARPE. Wilt.

- **Compréhension globale**

I. Fill in the grid with the information about the status (dog, wife, pupils, hero) *of each character in the story and say whether they are actually present* (yes) *or simply referred to* (no).

	Status	Present
1. Henry		
2. Eva		
3. Clem		
4. Gasfitters		

---

2. wishful thinking: acting as if something is true or will happen.
3. putative: supposed to be.
4. lotus position: a yoga position.

II. Select the appropriate starting point on the street map and draw the route that Henry Wilt always took.

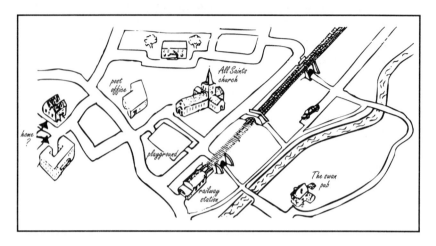

• **Compréhension détaillée**

I. Choose the word or phrase which best corresponds to the quotation.

1. . . . . . . he would only be able to <u>fulfil</u> his latent promise (1.25).
   a) forget   b) carry out   c) express.
2. . . . . . . he would be <u>doomed</u> to . . . . . . rest of his life (1.38-40).
   a) condemned to   b) able to escape   c) happy to stay with.
3. . . . . . . it was not a prospect to be <u>borne</u> (1.40).
   a) he was bored with the prospect.
   b) he enjoyed the prospect.
   c) he couldn't put up with the prospect.

II. Say whether the following statements are right or wrong, and justify with a quotation from the text. An indication is given as to the approximate number of words or lines expected.

1. Wilt would rather be Prime Minister than Minister of Education.
   (4 words)
2. Wilt was a remarkable-looking man.
   (7 words)
3. Wilt was convinced he would always be a failure unless his wife were eliminated.
   (2 lines)
4. Wilt found it easy to make up his mind.
   (6 words)

5. Wilt occupied a top position at work.
   (4 words)
6. Discipline was never a problem at the Fenland Tech.
   (4 words)
7. Wilt was delighted at the prospect of teaching Gasfitter apprentices for the rest of his career.
   (5 words)
8. Wilt was pretty sure of getting a promotion this year at last.
   (2 lines)

III. The following words reflect Wilt's states of mind between lines 1 and 27. Note beside each one the number of the line referring to it.

1. submission
2. uneasiness
3. envy
4. dreaming
5. delusions of grandeur
6. imaginary conversations
7. murderous thoughts

IV. Read this description of Wilt. It contains 7 mistakes. Pick out the words or expressions that are wrong. Justify their inaccuracy with quotations from the text.

Henry Wilt had worked for ten years as a Senior Lecturer in Liberal Studies at a prestigious university. He was married to a woman he loved, possessed a Yorkshire terrier called Eva, and had a friend called Clem who was a businessman. He would have liked, on occasion, to occupy a high position in the government and was keen on yoga. He lived in a house in a high-class residential district. While walking the dog he would talk to himself.

C. EXPRESSION PERSONNELLE

I. Expression semi-guidée (about 150 words).

In his secret diary, Wilt expresses his frustrations, his deepest wishes and ambitions...

II. Expression libre (about 250 words).

Choose one subject.

1. "Teaching is a vocation". Do you agree?
2. Is ambition necessary in life?

CORRIGÉS

A. COMPÉTENCE LINGUISTIQUE

I

1. How long have you been singing?
2. Which kind of music would you rather play?
3. How often do you go?
4. Whose guitars are these?
5. How much do you earn?/does it cost?

II

1. Whatever the student may say, the teacher was suspicious.
2. The authorities sent five helicopters so that all the families could be evacuated from the flood.
3. Unless someone helps me, I'll never be ready on time.
4. He brings back a present for his wife whenever he goes to London.
5. The pilot insisted on taking off in spite of bad wheather conditions.

III

1. The fire brigade should be called immediately.
2. A new fast-food restaurant is being built near our house.
3. She was prevented from going home early by the exam dates.

IV

1. It's been three years since I last saw him.
2. I whish I didn't have to go now.
3. There's nothing to see/ nothing to be seen.
4. It's no use complaining to the police about the noise your neighbours make.
5. It's time we made a decision.
6. You needn't write such a letter.
7. They must have seen the burglar break into the house.

V + VI

1. can be found.
2. have traveled (since 1978).
3. have returned.
4. will be (within the next decade).
5. is promising (now).
6. earns.
7. addressed (last month).
8. welcomed.
9. was (even if).
10. would be (if I returned).

B. COMPRÉHENSION D'UN TEXTE ÉCRIT

● **Compréhension globale**

I

	Status	present
1. Henry	hero	yes
2. Eva	wife	yes
3. Clem	dog	yes
4. Gasfitters	pupils	no

II

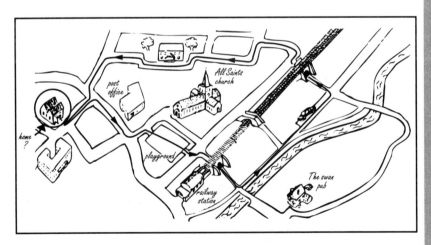

● **Compréhension détaillée**

I

1. b) carry out
2. a) condemned to
3. c) he couldn't put up with the prospect

II

1. RIGHT
   "better still, Prime Minister".
2. WRONG
   "anybody noticing Wilt (and most people didn't)".
3. RIGHT
   "...Wilt first conceived the notion that he would only be able to fulfil his latent promise and call his life his own if some not entirely fortuitous disaster overtook his wife".
4. WRONG
   "it was not a sudden decision".
5. WRONG
   "Assistant Lecturer (Grade Two)".
6. WRONG
   "or keeping them quiet".
7. WRONG
   "it was not a prospect to be borne".
8. WRONG
   "...his application to be promoted to Senior Lecturer was almost certain to be turned down".

III

1. submission: 1.2-3
2. uneasiness: 1.12
3. envy: 1.13
4. dreaming: 1.16
5. delusions of grandeur: 1.17-18
6. imaginary conversations: 1.19-23
7. murderous thoughts: 1.26-29

IV

1. as a Senior Lecturer: "as an Assistant Lecturer".
2. a prestigious university: "Fenland College of Arts and Technology (the Tech)".
3. a woman he loved: "wishful thinking, involving the irrevocable disappearance of Mrs. Wilt".
4. a Yorkshire terrier called Eva: "Clem, a pedigree Labrador".
5. a friend called Clem who was a businessman: "Clem, a pedigree Labrador".
6. was keen on yoga: "To escape from the memory [...] of Eva in the lotus position".
7. in a high-class residential district: "back through streets where the houses were bigger than Wilts's semi".

C. EXPRESSION PERSONNELLE

I. Expression semi-guidée

Took Clem for the usual walk tonight. Just when I was thinking of the way I'd redesign the admission scheme to college, he had to stop right in front of Mrs Proderick-Jones's mansion to do a number two. The old cow was staring at us disapprovingly from a French window, she looked distinctly like Eva except maybe uglier still if this were possible. Which brings me back to my domestic tyrant. I can't wait for the parcel to arrive in the post, they said their rat poison was 100% failure-proof, which should make for a few happy years. Just me and Clem! What with the money from the inheritance – and her cousins had better not meddle with this–, I could take a holiday in the Bahamas; when I get back, I must apply for Crimpton's job, then the Tech will see that I mean business. Better start writing my application right away.

II. Expression libre

1. Being a teacher can't be easy. I wonder what it feels like to be standing right in front of thirty-odd children or teenagers. However, most of my teachers seem to be coping quite well, apart from the occasional fit of temper! Actually, they largely seem to enjoy their job, so they must feel a genuine vocation for it. How else could you explain the way they put up with the various kinds of pressure their job entails? True, they enjoy longer holidays than anybody else, but they also have very few career incentives: internal promotion is limited and their salary is comparatively low; the average engineer (let alone a doctor) earns twice as much as a teacher for a comparable level of qualification. Another argument commonly levelled at teachers is their easy schedule: "You mean, you teach fifteen or eighteen hours a week and you call that *work?*" What many people overlook is the amount of time spent preparing for classes and marking papers, which surely brings the average teacher's schedule to a good forty- or fifty-hour week, a perfectly decent amount by any standards! Besides, there is the nervous tension of communicating with relatively large groups of people: the "blackboard jungle" applies to the teacher as much as it does to the students; performing in front of a class is a form of theater, but of the least rewarding kind: you never get any applause or rave reviews, the gratification you derive from your job has to come from yourself. Then again, some teachers might well be frustrated actors in the first place, thereby displaying a kind of transferred vocation!

2. Ambition is often looked down upon as a symptom of self-agrandizing. In my view, this confuses ambition, which is no evil in itself, with sheer vanity. Far from being a form of self-delusion, ambition begins with a cool-headed assessment of your own limitations in order for you to overcome them. For example, you may be too slow a runner, or not very good at algebra; you have to take stock of this before you can do anything about it and start setting yourself new goals. In this sense, ambition is merely the desire to fulfil one's potential to the best of one's abilities. Indeed, if you were not ambitious, you would never get anything done: why bother to go on studying once you've graduated from high school? Why put oneself to the trouble of talking to someone you fancy? Why enter a training scheme to get promotion at work? You might as well lie in bed all day, which certainly is not my attitude to life! However, I do not approve of ruthless go-getters either. Some people will develop their ambition at other people's expense, feeling no qualms about wrecking a colleague's career or letting their family life take second place to their jobs. This form of ambition I would call plain narrow-mindedness, inasmuch as it distorts one's goals and ultimately leads to personal failure. What is the use of becoming rich and famous if your inner self has to suffer for it? Ultimately, you cannot avoid some central ethical questions: what do you call a worthwhile goal? Only when you have answered this question may you feel entitled to throwing all your energies into the pursuit you have set for yourself.

SUJET

S 54

A. COMPÉTENCE LINGUISTIQUE

I. Entourez la lettre correspondant à la bonne réponse.

1. There were . . . . people present, they had to cancel the meeting.
   a) too much   b) too many   c) too few   d) very little.

2. The Robinsons couldn't afford a skiing vacation, they hadn't got . . . . . .
   . . . . . . money.
   a) enough   b) some   c) so much   d) no.

3. Your sister hasn't been . . . . successful as you have, she didn't pass.
   a) as   b) as much   c) so much   d) more.

4. Paul and Mary looked at . . . . and finally came to an agreement.
   a) themselves   b) each other   c) them   d) each one.

5. He asked me to choose between two solutions, but I agreed to
   . . . .
   a) either   b) neither   c) other   d) each other.

6. He's very obstinate; . . . . can make him change his mind.
   a) everybody   b) anybody   c) nobody   d) somebody.

II. Complétez à l'aide des mots tirés de la liste ci-dessous :

which - what - of which - whose - where - when - how - whenever - why - whereas - that.

1. I remember the time . . . . my grandmother was still alive.

2. She was so embarrassed she didn't know . . . . to say.

3. The car . . . . crashed into mine wasn't insured.

4. . . . . I meet a black cat, I cross my fingers.

5. Could you find out . . . . suitcase this is ?

6. I'm tall and thin . . . . my sister is rather short and fat.

7. It's incredible . . . . badly these children behave !

8. . . . . one of you has hidden my glasses again ?

III. Entourez a, b ou c afin d'obtenir une phrase correcte.

1. The burglar who broke into my flat . . . . left his finger prints everywhere !
   a) must have been
   b) shouldn't have
   c) had better

2. I was badly injured in this car crash, but it . . . . worse !
   a) must have been
   b) shouldn't be
   c) might have been

3. He would never have recognized me if I . . . . told him my name.
   a) should have
   b) hadn't
   c) can't have.

4. It's going to rain, you . . . . hurry if you don't want to get soaked.
   a) had better
   b) shouldn't
   c) would rather not

IV. Reformulez les phrases suivantes en utilisant les amorces fournies.

1. I've never witnessed such a destructive hurricane.
   This is . . . .

2. Samantha hasn't seen her relatives from Australia for at least ten years.
   It is ten years. . . . .

3. They often tell him not to smoke so much.
   He is . . . .

4. A baby-sitter looks after the children once a week.
   The children . . . .

5. It isn't necessary for you to remind me all the time to watch my language !
   I needn't . . . .

6. The President is expected to make a speech tonight.
   Everybody. . . . .

B. COMPRÉHENSION D'UN TEXTE ÉCRIT

The Last of the Caddoes

By the shores of the Red River, in Texas, lived a boy named Jimmy Hawkins, who learned one day to his surprise that he was, on his father's side, part Indian. Until then Jimmy had always thought he was just another white boy.

5 A curious reluctance had kept Jimmy's mother from ever telling him about his Indian blood. She had felt it from the time he first began to question her about himself, about the family. She shied away from it

warily, almost as though in fear. This was very silly of her, of course.
Just childishness. Some old bogeyman left over from her early child-
10 hood, nothing more. She had never seen a live Indian in her life. The
savages, even in Texas, had long since been pacified, not to say exterminated. Being afraid of Indians in those days and times, when the only
ones left were celluloid Indians, Saturday-matinee horse-opera Indians!
[...]
15 Yet all the while Jimmy's mother felt she really perhaps ought to just
mention it. There were times, indeed, when it was as though she were
being urged from all sides to tell him, reproached for her silence, even
almost commanded to speak out without further delay. "But what on
earth difference does it make?" she would argue. "Nowadays what dif-
20 ference does it make? None whatever." Though in fact it might have
made a great difference to Jimmy. The boy was simply crazy about
Indians: read about nothing else, dressed himself up as one, made himself beadwork belts, sewed his own moccasins; his mother might have
guessed that to be able to claim he was part Indian would have pleased
25 him as nothing else could. [...]
It came out unexpectedly one day when they were having one of their
rows. Lately it had gotten so all they ever did, it seemed, was fuss and
quarrel. Jimmy was passing through a difficult phase. Going on thirteen
now, and feeling new powers stirring within him, he was forever testing
30 his strength, trying his mother, seeing just how far he could go, how much
he could get away with. This one was their third fight in two days.
Jimmy had done something he knew not to do, had been scolded and
punished, and had turned sullen and defiant. His punishment would end,
he was told, when he confessed he had been bad and said he was sorry;
35 the set of his jaw proclaimed that he had vowed he would sooner die. He
could be very stubborn.
He grew bolder and more impudent until at last he said something so
sassy she slapped his face. This made dart from Jimmy's black eyes two
poisoned arrows of hatred. "Oh!" cried his mother, pierced by his look,
40 "I don't know what gets into you at times like this!" Then before she
knew it, "It must be the Indian in you coming out."

William Humphrey "The Last of the Caddoes"
in *A Time and a Place.* Ed. A. Knopf, New York, 1968.

- **Compréhension globale**

I. What genre does the text belong to? (Tick the right answer.)

    a) purely fictional
    b) historical
    c) fictional with a historical background
    d) thriller

II. Circle the letter corresponding to the best statement.

1. The text is mostly about:

a) the extermination of the American Indians
b) a boy's teenage crisis
c) a woman's inability to raise her child
d) the issue of identity.

2. The title "The last of the Caddoes" refers to:
   a) Jimmy's family name
   b) an old bogeyman
   c) Jimmy himself
   d) Jimmy's father.

3. This story is narrated by:
   a) Jimmy
   b) an objective external narrator
   c) Jimmy's mother
   d) an Indian from Texas.

4. The revelation made at the end of the text is:
   a) a mere lie
   b) just a joke
   c) aimed at the boy
   d) here to inform the reader about a new element.

III. Give the right number (from 1 to 6) to the following sentences, according to the progression of the text.

(...) The constant struggle between mother and son,
(...) We learn that Jimmy Hawkins has got Indian blood,
(...) The mother's strong desire to reveal the truth,
(...) The reasons for the mother's fear to inform her son,
(...) The final disclosure of the truth,
(...) Some hints about Jimmy's interest in Indian culture.

● **Compréhension détaillée**

I. Circle RIGHT or WRONG and justify by a short quotation from the text.

1. Jimmy suspected he had Indian blood.   RIGHT - WRONG
   . . . .

2. His mother had never told him the truth.   RIGHT - WRONG
   . . . .

3. Some Indians lived in their community.   RIGHT - WRONG
   . . . .

4. Deep inside herself the mother wanted to tell him.   RIGHT - WRONG
   . . . .

5. Jimmy didn't want to have anything to do with
   Indians.   RIGHT - WRONG
   . . . .

6. After having thought about it for a long time, she
finally told him.   RIGHT - WRONG
. . . .

7. They quarrelled at least once a day.   RIGHT - WRONG
. . . .

8. He refused to apologize.   RIGHT - WRONG
. . . .

*II. For each of the following statements, find two equivalents in the text
(short sentences or expressions).*

1. She carefully avoided the subject.
. . . .

2. Something compelled her to reveal the truth to him.
. . . .

3. He was a great fan of Indian culture.
. . . .

4. As a teenager he gave his mother a hard time.
. . . .

III. Say to what words the following pronouns stand for (quote the text).

1. It (She had felt it . . . .) (line 6)
. . . .

2. It (. . . . . . . she really perhaps ought to just mention it . . . . .) (l. 15-16).
. . . .

3. One (. . . . . dressed himself up as one . . . .) (l. 22).
. . . .

4. It (. . . . . it had gotten so . . . .) (l. 27).
. . . .

5. One (This one was their third fight . . . .) (l. 31).
. . . .

6. It (It must be the Indian in you . . . .) (l. 41).
. . . .

IV. Translate the following sentences.

1. His punishment would end, he was told, when he confessed he had been
bad and said he was sorry.

2. This made dart from Jimmy's black eyes two poisoned arrows of hatred.

C. EXPRESSION PERSONNELLE

I. Production semi-guidée (about 150 words).

Imagine Jimmy's reaction after he has been told the truth, his new feelings about himself and towards his mother. Speak in the first person.

II. Production libre (about 200 words).

Traitez *l'un des deux sujets* suivants :

1. Recent books and films have expressed a renewal of interest in the culture of the American Indian. Can you explain the reason for this new concern ?
2. How important is it to know one's origins and identity ? Discuss this issue by giving examples.

CORRIGÉS

A. COMPÉTENCE LINGUISTIQUE

I

1. too few.
2. enough.
3. as.
4. each other.
5. neither.
6. nobody.

II

1. when.
2. what.
3. that.
4. Whenever.
5. whose.
6. whereas.
7. how.
8. Which.

III

1. shouldn't have.
2. might have been.
3. hadn't.

4. had better.

IV

1. This is the most destructive hurricane I have ever witnessed.
2. It is ten years since Samantha saw her relatives from Australia.
3. He is often told not to smoke so much.
4. The children are looked after by a baby-sitter once a week.
5. I needn't be reminded to watch my language all the time.
6. Everybody expects the President to make a speech tonight.

B. COMPRÉHENSION D'UN TEXTE ÉCRIT

● **Compréhension globale**

I

c) fictional with a historical background.

II

1. b) a boy's teenage crisis (or c: a woman's inability to raise her child).
2. c) Jimmy himself.
3. b) an objective external narrator.
4. c) aimed at the boy.

III

The constant struggle between mother and son: §4.
We learn that Jimmy Hawkins has got Indian blood: §1.
The mother's strong desire to reveal the truth: §3 (beginning).
The reasons for the mother's fear to inform her son: §2.
The final disclosure of the truth: §5.
Some hints about Jimmy's interest in Indian culture: §3 (end).

● **Compréhension détaillée**

I

1. WRONG
"...who learned one day to his surprise".
2. RIGHT

"...had kept Jimmy's mother from ever telling him..."
3. WRONG
"The only ones left were celluloid Indians".
4. RIGHT
"There were times [...] when it was as though she were being urged from all sides to tell him."
5. WRONG
"The boy was simply crazy about Indians."
6. WRONG
"It came out unexpectedly;"
7. RIGHT
"This one was their third fight in two days."
8. RIGHT
"...the set of his jaw proclaimed that he had vowed he would sooner die".

II

1. "She shied away from it".
   "A curious reluctance had kept [her] from ever telling him".
2. "[She] felt she really perhaps just ought to mention it".
   "...as though she were being urged [...] to tell him".
3. "[He] was crazy about Indians."
   "...to claim he was part Indian would have pleased him."
4. "Jimmy was passing through a difficult phase."
   "Going on thirteen now [...] he was forever [...] trying his mother".

III

1. it = telling him about his Indian blood.
2. it = his Indian blood/the fact he had Indian blood/the truth.
3. one = an Indian.
4. it = Jimmy's attitude to his mother/his relationship with her.
5. one = row.
6. it = what gets into you at times like this.

IV

1. Sa punition serait levée, lui fit-elle savoir, lorsqu'il aurait reconnu qu'il avait été vilain et qu'il aurait demandé pardon.
2. Cela fit jaillir des yeux noirs de Jimmy deux flèches de haine venimeuses.

C. EXPRESSION PERSONNELLE

I. Expression semi-guidée

Talk about a revelation! Why didn't she tell me earlier? Maybe she was scared I might start behaving like an Indian and would cut their throats in the middle of the night. Now what? Does this mean I can dress up as an Indian every day of the week? I'm not even sure what Indians do these days. Don't think I've actually ever met one. No wonder she wouldn't tell me about Pop's ancestry, I bet she's ashamed of it. She's always acted funny around me as if I were different somehow. Well, now I know. I wonder which tribe Pop's ancestors belonged to, she wouldn't say or maybe she just doesn't know, she couldn't care less. I wouldn't mind being a Seminole or a Cherokee. Maybe I still have fullblood Indian relatives. That would be something! I could go and live with them on a reservation, I wouldn't have to tell a soul. I must go and look up the nearest reservation in the public library.

II. Expression libre

1. American Indians, or Native Americans as they are called these days, are a thorn in the side of America's good conscience; after all, they were ruthlessly expropriated and exterminated by white settlers in the nineteenth century, before becoming a commonplace of the American collective unconscious, in the guise of Westerns and rodeos. A change occured in the late sixties, with the first truly modern depiction of the plight of Indian tribes in films such as *Soldier Blue* or *A Man Named Horse*. At the same time, hippies adopted a few artifacts of Indian dress, such as headbands and fringe jackets. Now, twenty-five years on, Native Americans are back at the forefront of popular culture with Jim Harrison and Tony Hillerman's novels and Kevin Costner's box-office success *Dance With Wolves*. And even if young people no longer feel the need to wear beads and bangles, there is a pervasive influence of Native American design on modern youth fashion, including Oxbow's popular line of sportswear. This renewal of interest may be ascribed to the current New Age fad, involving as it does a quest for spiritual values in an increasingly materialistic world. Native Americans have come to represent for us, as they once did for Rousseau, the embodiment of a life at one with nature. For lack of more credible models, and because we tend to over-romanticize the exotic, many people turn to the more superficial aspects of Native American cultures. Unfortunately, this is just not enough to redress the wrongs committed by our (or their) forefathers, and it can in no way replace a serious commitment to the welfare of today's Native Americans.

2. Many people take their identity or their origins for granted, assuming that their ancestors hailed from a limited area. However, this is definitely not true of second- or third-generation immigrants, who live at one remove from their roots without necessarily feeling fully integrated into their country of residence. My North-African friends are as French as anybody else, but they still talk with longing about "home", their grandparents' village in the Atlas or their cousin's beach house near Agadir. And yet, they acknowledge quite openly that they wouldn't dream of moving back to their forefathers' place as it holds few private memories for them. They enjoy spending their holidays there but that is about as far as it goes. Some of them are also devoted Coranic students, and they try to make the best of both worlds without repudiating either their family's past or the Western culture around them.

I have another friend who was told only quite recently that she had been adopted, and as a result she has decided to go hunting for her roots. She said she would never reject her foster parents, but at the same time she needs to find out more about her biological parents in order to know herself better, which is something I can understand. She also said that she would probably adopt children herself some day whether she had children of her own or not, and she will do everything in her power to help them find out more about their past. Ultimately, it seems essential to know where you are coming from in so far as it enables you to chart a route for yourself.

SUJET

A. COMPÉTENCE LINGUISTIQUE

I. Mettez les verbes entre parenthèses à la forme et au temps appropriés (changez l'ordre des mots si nécessaire) :

1. If I were you, I (tell) .... him what to do.

2. I'd rather you (not go) .... out tonight.

3. Why you (not leave) .... straight away? Then you are sure to arrive on time.

4. If she (be) .... more helpful, I would have liked her more.

5. How about (go) .... to the pictures tonight?

6. He was meant (repair) .... his car himself.

7. It is the first time she (have) .... a dress made by a tailor.

8. (You not notice) .... anyone near the building when the bomb went off?

9. They (walk) .... for a long time when at last they saw a sign-post.

10. I heard someone (slam) .... the door, and then there was silence.

II. Complétez le passage ci-dessous à l'aide de la liste suivante :

"what, which, when, where, whose, that, ∅":

The young man .... name I can't remember, told me about an unfortunate accident .... had happened to him. I don't know .... or .... it took place, but he said .... the only thing .... mattered to him was his car. .... he had not foreseen was .... it would be completely smashed one day. All .... is so sad .... I can hardly believe it.

III. *Construisez cinq phrases cohérentes en utilisant pour chaque phrase un élément de chacune des trois colonnes :*

1. Paul had to sell his car	in order to	he desperately needs some money.
2. The government poured money into rural development	as long as	buy a house abroad.
3. He will not be able to go abroad for a holiday	although	improve the quality of life in the country.
4. I will live happily	so as to	he saves up a lot of money.
5. He refuses to sell his car	unless	I can do what I like.

IV. *Complétez les phrases à l'aide d'un modal pris dans la liste suivante (can, can't, may, might, couldn't, must, should, ought to, needn't, dared), chacun ne pouvant être utilisé qu'une fois, et transformez le verbe entre parenthèses si nécessaire :*

1. You (do) .... the shopping now; tomorrow will do.

2. Since she isn't here, I'm sure she (forget) .... about the meeting.

3. I was so surprised that I (say) .... a word.

4. She (commit) .... the murder; she has an alibi.

5. The weather forecast says it (rain) .... this afternoon.

6. Before letting everybody else know about it, you (tell) .... your parents first.

7. He overcame his fear, and for once he (oppose) .... his father.

8. He said that he (fall) .... asleep at the wheel, but he really did not remember the cause of the accident.

9. When you (deliver) .... the goods?

10. Why didn't you come? You (come) .... at once.

V. *Réécrivez les phrases suivantes sans en changer le sens, en commençant par l'amorce proposée :*

1. If anything happened to him, I would be upset.

   Should ....

2. He doesn't like coffee or whisky.

   He likes ....

60

3. I cannot see him anywhere..

   He . . . .

4. I like playing golf – me too.

   I like playing golf – . . . .

5. Whatever he does he will succeed.

   No matter . . . .

6. How about changing your mind?

   I suggest . . . .

7. I regret having left so early.

   I wish . . . .

8. "Can I use your dictionary?"

   She asked me . . . .

9. "I will go to England next year".

   He thought . . . .

10. The headmaster was telling the boys off.

    The boys . . . .

B. COMPRÉHENSION D'UN TEXTE ÉCRIT

Marian was walking slowly down the aisle, keeping pace with the gentle music that swelled and rippled around her. " Beans '', she said. She found the kind marked "Vegetarian'' and tossed two cans into her wire cart.

5   The music swung into a tinkly waltz; she proceeded down the aisle, trying to concentrate on her list. She resented the music because she knew why it was there : it was supposed to lull you into a euphoric trance, lower your sales resistance to the point at which all things are desirable. But just because she knew what they were up to didn't mean
10   she was immune. These days, if she wasn't careful, she found herself pushing the cart like a somnambulist, eyes fixed, swaying slightly, her hands twitching with the impulse to reach out and grab anything with a bright label. She had begun to defend herself with lists, willing herself to buy nothing, however deceptively priced or subliminally packaged,
15   except what was written there. When she was feeling unusually susceptible she would tick the things off the list with a pencil as an additional countercharm.

But in some ways they would always be successful : they couldn't miss. You had to buy something sometime. She knew enough about it
20   from the office to realize that the choice between, for instance, two brands of soap or two cans of tomato juice was not what could be called a rational one. In the products there was no real difference. How did you choose then? You could only abandon yourself to the soothing music and make a random snatch.

25   She steered her cart towards the vegetable area and picked listlessly
through the vegetables. She used to be fond of a good salad but now she
had to eat so many of them she was beginning to find them tiresome.
How she longed to become again a carnivore, to gnaw on a good bone !
Christmas dinner had been difficult. "Why Marian, you're not eating !"
30 her mother had fussed when she had left the turkey untouched on her
plate. She had said she wasn't hungry, and had eaten huge quantities of
cranberry sauce and mashed potatoes when no one was looking. Her
mother had set her strange loss of appetite down to overexcitement. She
had thought of saying she had taken up a new religion that forbade her
35 to eat meat, but it wouldn't have been a good idea : they had been pathe-
tically eagger to have the wedding in the family church. Their reaction
though, as far as she could estimate the reactions of people who were
now so remote from her, was less elated glee[1] than a quiet, rather smug
satisfaction, as though their fears about the effects of her university edu-
40 cation, never stated but always apparent, had been calmed at last. They
had probably been worried she would turn into a high-school teacher or
a maiden aunt or a dope addict or a female executive. But now, their
approving eyes said, she was turning out all right after all.

Margaret Atwood, *The Edible Woman.*

• **Compréhension globale**

I. What is the setting of

1. the first part ? . . . .
2. the second part ? . . . .

*II. In the following pairs circle the letter corresponding to the correct state-
ment.*

1. As Marian did her shopping
   a) she enjoyed the music
   b) she disliked the music

2. When Marian left school
   a) she immediately got an office job
   b) she went to university

3. Marian is at present unmarried
   a) but she is about to get married
   b) and she intends to stay single

4. a) Marian has always been a vegetarian
   b) formerly Marian was not a vegetarian

---

1. elated glee : a feeling of great joy and excitement.

- **Compréhension détaillée**

I. Right or Wrong? Circle the letter R ou W, and justify your answer by quoting from the text.

1. Marian knew that the music in shops made people buy more.   R - W
   . . . .

2. She herself was able to resist its influence.   R - W
   . . . .

3. She crossed the items off her list to make sure she had not forgotten anything.   R - W
   . . . .

4. She was no longer keen on eating salads.   R - W
   . . . .

5. Her mother knew she was a vegetarian.   R - W
   . . . .

6. Marian did not have much appetite for Christmas dinner.   R - W
   . . . .

7. She told her family that she had changed her religion.   R - W
   . . . .

8. She felt out of touch with her family.   R - W
   . . . .

9. They had said that they were afraid of the bad influence of a university education.   R - W
   . . . .

10. Her family thought that a woman who had a career but no husband was a failure.   R - W
   . . . .

II. Circle the letter corresponding to the right answer.

1. "keeping pace with the gentle music" means
    a) listening hard to the gentle music
    b) moving in time to the gentle music
    c) feeling peaceful because of the gentle music
2. "she knew what they were up to" means
    a) she was aware of their intentions
    b) she knew how far they had got
    c) she knew what they were capable of
3. "make a random snatch" means
    a) seize any product at all
    b) take the most attractive product
    c) choose the nearest product

4. "she was turning out all right" means
   a) she was looking prettier and prettier
   b) she was becoming a more likeable person
   c) she was proving to be successful

III. Quote 2 phrases that show

1. that Marian considers shopping to be a sort of war in which she is on the weaker side.
   ....
   ....
2. that the music in shops turns people into unthinking zombies.
   ....
   ....

IV. Find the words in the text with the same meaning as :

- a bit : ....
- to fail : ....
- to want very much : ....
- to attribute to : ....
- far away : ....
- to become : ....

C. EXPRESSION PERSONNELLE

I. Production semi-guidée (100 to 150 words).

Write a dialogue between Marian, who expresses her preference for vegetarian food, and her parents, who reproach her with being a vegetarian and try to make her change her mind.

II. Production libre (200 to 250 words).

Traitez l'un des deux sujets suivants.

1. Is it possible for a woman to combine a successful career with having a husband and children ? What are the advantages and drawbacks both for her and her family ?
2. Do you find shopping to be a pleasurable activity or a nightmare ? Justify your point of view.

CORRIGÉS

A. *COMPÉTENCE LINGUISTIQUE*

I

1. would tell.	6. to repair.
2. did not go.	7. has had.
3. don't you leave.	8. hadn't you noticed / didn't you notice.
4. had been.	9. had been walking.
5. going.	10. slam.

II

The young man <u>whose</u> name I can't remember told me about an unfortunate accident <u>which</u> had happened to him. I don't know <u>where</u> or <u>when</u> it took place, but he said <u>that/∅</u> the only thing <u>that</u> mattered to him was his car. <u>What</u> he had not foreseen was <u>that</u> it would be completely smashed one day. All <u>that</u> is so sad <u>that/∅</u> I can hardly believe it.

III

1. Paul had to sell his car so as to buy a house abroad.
2. The government poured money into rural development in order to improve the quality of life in the country.
3. He will not be able to go abroad for a holiday unless he saves up a lot of money.
4. I will live happily as long as I can do what I like.
5. He refuses to sell his car although he desperately needs some money.

IV

1. needn't.
2. must have forgotten.
3. couldn't say.
4. can't have committed.
5. might rain.
6. ought to tell.
7. dared oppose.
8. must have fallen.
9. can you deliver.
10. should have come.

V

1. Should anything happen to him, I would be upset.
2. He likes neither coffee nor whisky.
3. He is not to be seen (He cannot be seen) anywhere.
4. So do I.
5. No matter what he does, he will succeed.
6. I suggest you (should) change your mind.
7. I wish I hadn't left so early.
8. She asked me if / whether she could use my dictionary.
9. He thought he would go to England the following year.
10. The boys were being told off by the headmaster.

B. COMPRÉHENSION D'UN TEXTE ÉCRIT

- **Compréhension globale**

I

1. a supermarket.
2. Christmas dinner at Marian's parents'.

II

1. b) she disliked the music.
2. b) she went to university.
3. a) but she is about to get married.
4. b) formerly Marian was not a vegetarian.

- **Compréhension détaillée**

I

1. RIGHT
"She resented the music because she knew why it was there: it was supposed to [...] lower your sales resistance".
2. WRONG
"But just because she knew what they were up to didn't mean she was immune".
3. WRONG
"When she was feeling unusually susceptible, she would tick the things off the list with a pencil as an additional countercharm".

4. RIGHT
"...now she had to eat so many of them she was beginning to find them tiresome".
5. WRONG
"Her mother had set her strange loss of appetite down to overexcitement".
6. WRONG
"She had said she wasn't hungry, and had eaten huge quantites of cranberry sauce and mashed potatoes when no one was looking."
7. WRONG
"She had thought of saying she had taken up a new religion [...] but it wouldn't have been a good idea."
8. RIGHT
"...as far as she could estimate the reaction of people who were now so remote from her".
9. WRONG
"...their fears about the effects of her university education, never stated but always apparent".
10. RIGHT
"They had probably been worried she might turn into a high-school teacher or a maiden aunt".

II

1. b) moving in time to gentle music.
2. a) she was aware of their intentions.
3. a) seize any product at all.
4. b) she was becoming a more likeable person.

III

1. "She had begun to defend hersef".
   "But in some ways they would always be successful: they couldn't miss".
2. "...it was supposed to lull you into a euphoric trance".
   "...she found herself pushing the cart like a somnambulist".

IV

a bit = slightly
to fail = to miss
to want very much = to long for
to attribute to = to set down to
far away = remote
to become = to turn into

C. EXPRESSION PERSONNELLE

I. Expression semi-guidée

(At the dinner table at Marian's parents'.)

MARIAN'S MOTHER: Marian, what's the matter with you? You've hardly eaten anything.

MARIAN: Nothing's the matter, Mum, it's just that I've given up meat.

MARIAN'S FATHER: You're not one of those veggies?

MARIAN: As a matter of fact, I am. And by the way, the word is *vegetarian,* not *veggie.*

MARIAN'S MOTHER: What's wrong with you?

MARIAN: Nothing, Mum. It's just that I'd rather not eat meat.

MARIAN'S FATHER: But why not? Meat is perfectly healthy food.

MARIAN: That's what *you* think. It's actually loaded with toxins, hormones and all kinds of disgusting chemicals. Beans and cereals are actually much healthier for you.

MARIAN'S MOTHER: So what am I supposed to cook for you? Sometimes you can be so selfish. Why don't you have a nice slice of roast beef?

MARIAN: Listen, Mum, I've just told you I've given up meat! It's no use trying to forcefeed me.

II. Expression libre

1. Many women today are working mothers: they manage to combine a career with a housewife's role. In the process, they earn some self-respect (not to mention their own income). Indeed, women's work was one of the battle horses of early feminists who were hoping to achieve some sense of independence. However, the number of women in the workplace has increased so much because of the two World Wars rather than in order to satisfy the suffragettes' demands: employers started hiring women for lack of a male workforce, and also because they thought women would accept lower wages than men. We are still heirs to that mentality: not only do women tend to have lesser-paid jobs than men, but above all many of them end up doing two jobs at once, one as a working person and the other as a housewife. As a result, some women are overtired and do not feel gratified. They end up doing neither job properly and blame themselves for it when in fact they are caught in a vicious circle beyond their control. For all this, I do not by any means advocate a return to the good old days of housebound women. Instead, it is a matter of husbands sharing the chores with their wives, and mothers teaching their children to do the house-work irrespective of sex. Besides, a lot remains to be done as far as employers are concerned in order to make it easier for mothers to combine a career with motherhood. In the end, we should all be the better for it.

2. I once saw a T-shirt which read: "I shop, therefore I am." While I could hardly claim this motto as mine, what with its consumerist over-tones, I must admit that there are forms of shopping that I do enjoy. For example, I quite like to browse around record shops or bookstores for hours even if I don't buy anything. This has earned me many a dirty look from shopkeepers but I couldn't care less: after all, the items are there to be handled and looked at, and moreover I can be quite a good buyer if I'm in the right mood. However, there are also forms of shopping which I heartily dislike. For example, the thought of going out to buy clothes sends me into fits of anxiety. When I do buy new clothes, I always do so on an impulse, because something in a shopwindow has caught my fancy, but I could never spend half a day tramping around clothes shops trying on ten different pairs of trousers. I suppose changing booths make me feel claustrophobic! Anyway, as a rule I very rarely set off on a deliberate spending spree of any kind, or if I do, it feels like a real chore. I'm much more prone to silly impulse purchases, which means I probably spend just as much as more deliberate buyers at the end of the day! Does this make me an irresponsible consumer? Excuse me, but I've just seen something in that window...

SUJET

A. COMPÉTENCE LINGUISTIQUE

I. Entourer le mot de chaque série qui se prononce différemment des autres.

DEAR / A TEAR / FEAR / TO TEAR / BEER
TO LIVE / RIPE / TO WIPE / WIDE / TIGHT
TOUGH / ROUGH / BLUFF / TO COUGH / ENOUGH
TO BOW / TO VOW / A BLOW / A COW / NOW.

II. Compléter avec les adjectifs ou les pronoms possessifs adéquats.

1. It can't be Christopher's bag: . . . . is much bigger.
2. This bird builds . . . . nest very close to the ground.
3. Has everybody bought . . . . tickets ?
4. I'm surprised David lent you . . . . car; I wouldn't have lent you . . . .

III. Reformuler les phrases suivantes en utilisant l'élément donné afin d'obtenir des énoncés similaires.

1. It's a pity I didn't see her.
   I wish . . . .
2. They are testing the new engine.
   The new engine. . . . .
3. They gave him instructions.
   He . . . .
4. I would prefer you to do it now.
   I'd rather . . . .
5. If you drive fast, you run a lot of risks.
   The faster . . . .

IV. Rapporter les propos ci-dessous en utilisant l'amorce proposée.

1. "I forgot to tell him".
   She said. . . . .
2. "Don't run so fast!"
   He told me . . . .
3. "Are you quite sure?"
   She asked me . . . .
4. "I won't tell anybody."
   He said . . . .
5. "Why didn't you take a taxi?"
   He asked me . . . .

V. Ajouter les "question-tags" appropriés aux énoncés suivants :

1. You've never tried that, ... ?
2. Let's go and see them, ... ?
3. You'd rather stay at home, ... ?
4. Everybody agreed with him, ... ?
5. You'll always love me, ... ?
6. She can hardly walk, ... ?

VI. Choisir parmi les termes ci-dessous pour relier les phrases suivantes :

so that   owing to   unless   provided   whether
therefore   whereas

1. He won't help you . . . . he is in a very good mood.
2. I didn't like the trip . . . . my wife did.
3. He put it in a safe place . . . . nobody would find it.
4. They'll give you something to eat . . . . you don't come back too late.

B. COMPRÉHENSION D'UN TEXTE ÉCRIT

By a great deal of pushing and squirming, always trying to look as though he were enjoying himself, Tod finally managed to break into the open. After rearranging his clothes, he went over to a parking lot and sat down on the low retaining wall that ran along the front of it.

5   New groups, whole families, kept arriving. He could see a change come over them as soon as they had become part of the crowd. Until they reached the line, they looked diffident, almost furtive, but the moment they had become part of it, they turned arrogant and pugnacious. It was a mistake to think them harmless curiosity seekers. They

10   were savage and bitter, especially the middle-aged and the old, and had
been made so by boredom and disappointment.

All their lives they had slaved at some kind of dull, heavy labor,
behind desks and counters, in the fields and at tedious machines of all
sorts, saving their pennies and dreaming of the leisure that would be
15   theirs when they had enough. Finally that day came. They could draw a
weekly income of ten or fifteen dollars. Where else should they go but
California, the land of sunshine and oranges?

Once there, they discovered that sunshine isn't enough. They get tired
of oranges, even of avocado pears and passion fruit. Nothing happens.
20   They don't know what to do with their time. They haven't the mental
equipment for leisure, the money nor the physical equipment for pleasure. Did they slave so long just to go on an occasional Iowa picnic?
What else is there? They watch the waves come in at Venice? There
wasn't any ocean where most of them came from, but after you've seen
25   one wave, you've seen them all. The same is true of the airplanes at
Glendale. If only a plane would crash once in a while so that they could
watch the passengers being consumed in a "holocaust of flame", as the
newspapers put it. But the planes never crash.

Their boredom becomes more and more terrible. They realize that
30   they've been tricked and burn with resentment. Every day of their lives
they read the newspapers and went to the movies. Both fed them on
lynchings, murder, sex crimes, explosions, wrecks, love nests, fires,
miracles, revolutions, wars. This daily diet made sophisticates of them.
The sun is a joke. Oranges can't titillate their jaded palates. Nothing can
35   ever be violent enough to make taut their slack minds and bodies. They
have been cheated and betrayed. They have slaved and saved for
nothing.

Tod stood up. During the ten minutes he had been sitting on the wall,
the crowd had grown thirty feet and he was afraid that his escape might
40   be cut off if he loitered much longer. He crossed to the other side of the
street and started back.

From *The Day of the Locust,*
by Nathanael West (1939).

- **Compréhension globale**

Tick the right answer

1. Tod is   a) right in the middle of the crowd;
               b) watching from a distance;
               c) parking his car.

2. Most of the people there live   a) in California;
                                        b) in Iowa;
                                        c) in Italy.

3. Venice, a town which is mentioned in the passage, is
    a) in the mountains;
    b) in the Pacific coast;
    c) in the countryside.

4. The narrator   a) feels very close to the crowd;

                    b) does not identify with the crowd;

                    c) wants us to admire the people in the crowd.

• **Compréhension appronfondie**

I. Write "WRONG" or "RIGHT" and justify your answer by quoting from the text.

1. It had not been difficult for Tod to get away from the crowd.

☐   . . . .

2. Being part of the crowd made people behave differently.

☐   . . . .

3. The people in the crowd all had white-collar jobs.

☐   . . . .

4. They were still fascinated by the Pacific Ocean.

☐   . . . .

5. Little by little, the crowd was thinning away.

☐   . . . .

II. Among the following, circle the three adjectives that best describe the crowd.

PATIENT   BLOOD-THIRSTY   FUNNY   AGGRESSIVE
PROUD   FRUSTRATED   PEACEFUL   SATISFIED

III. Pick out three elements that account for the resentment and the bitterness the people in the crowd feel (from line 29 to the end).

IV. In the text find equivalents for the following words or expressions (use noun for noun, adverb for adverb, etc.).

Examples. • A lot → a great deal.
               • Having a good time → enjoying himself.
Twisting about like a bird: (lines 1 to 9) . . . .
Eager to fight: (lines 1 to 11) . . . .
Monotonous, not exciting: (lines 9 to 16, two answers) . . . .
. . . .
From time to time, now and then: (lines 24 to 33). . . . .
Weak, lacking in energy: (lines 33 to the end). . . . .

V. Translate the last paragraph into French (from "Tod stood up" to the end).

C. EXPRESSION PERSONNELLE

I. Expression semi-guidée (150 words).

Two persons in the crowd start talking. They *complain* about their lives and evoke their *regrets* and *expectations*.
Use relevant expressions and underline them.

II. Expression libre (250 words).

Traiter l'un des deux sujets suivants :
1. What are your views on violence in T.V. programmes ?
2. "United we stand, divided we fall." Discuss.

CORRIGÉS

A. *COMPÉTENCE LINGUISTIQUE*

I

to tear
to live
to cough
a blow

II

1. his.   2. its.   3. their.   4. his; mine.

III

1. I wish I had seen her.
2. The new engine is being tested.
3. He was given instructions.
4. I'd rather you did it now.
5. The faster you drive, the more risks you run.

IV

1. She said she had forgotten to tell me.

2. He told me not to run so fast.
3. She asked me if (= whether) I was quite sure.
4. He said he wouldn't tell anybody.
5. He asked me why I hadn't taken a taxi.

V

1. have you?
2. shall we?
3. wouldn't you?
4. didn't they?
5. won't you?
6. can she?

VI

1. unless.
2. whereas.
3. so that.
4. provided.

B. COMPRÉHENSION D'UN TEXTE ÉCRIT

● **Compréhension globale**

1. b) watching from a distance.
2. a) in California.
3. b) on the Pacific coast.
4. b) does not identify with the crowd.

● **Compréhension approfondie**

I

1. WRONG
"By a great deal of pushing and squirming [...] Tod finally managed to break into the open".
2. RIGHT
"He could see a change come over them as soon as they had become part of the crowd".
3. WRONG
"All their lives they had slaved at some kind of dull, heavy labor, behind desks and counters, in the fields and at tedious machines of all sorts".

4. WRONG

"...after you've seen one wave, you've seen them all".

5. WRONG

"...the crowd had grown thirty feet and he was afraid that his escape might be cut off if he loitered much longer".

II

aggressive / proud / frustrated.

III

1. Their boredom becomes more and more terrible.
2. They realize that they've been tricked and burn with resentment.
3. Oranges can't titillate a jaded palate.
4. Nothing can ever be violent enough to make taut their slack minds and bodies.
5. They have been cheated and betrayed.
6. They have slaved and saved for nothing.

IV

twisting about like a bird: squirming
eager to fight: pugnacious
monotonous, not exciting: dull / tedious
from time to time, now and then: once in a while
weak, lacking in energy: slack

V

Tod se leva. Pendant les dix minutes qu'il avait passées assis sur le muret, la foule avait gagné dix mètres et il avait peur de ne plus pouvoir passer s'il tardait trop. Il traversa la rue et repartit en sens inverse.

C. EXPRESSION PERSONNELLE

I. Expression semi-guidée

TOM: Why aren't I getting more out of life?

HARRY: You tell me! I came here hoping to find the good life, and look at me now. The missus keeps complaining that I don't bring in enough money, this mortgage is killing me.

Tom: Yeah, <u>I wish</u> I'd stayed back on the farm in Kentucky too. <u>I shouldn't have</u> listened to my brother when he told me to come and join him in California. Everything's <u>so dull</u> here. <u>I can't stand</u> the blue sky any more.

Harry: At least we're making money.

Tom: Right, but money ain't all. Surely <u>there's more to life than this</u>.

Harry: <u>Something's gotta break</u>. I wanted freedom and I've never felt so fenced in in my whole life. <u>I'm even looking forward to</u> that war that's all over the papers. <u>I'd give anything for a change</u>.

II. Expression libre

1. After major psychological studies highlighted the relationship between violence on TV and aggressive behaviour, many people started to worry about the impact of violent TV programmes. Some individuals would even go so far as to ban any kind of violence on TV. The obvious danger is that we might develop a kind of underhand censorship. Where do you draw the line between what is acceptable and what is not, and who is to decide? Of course, this is a burning issue mostly because TV is available to all and sundry, unlike films or books. You don't have to go out or pay any extra charge, all you need is to press a button or fiddle with your remote control. Parents may thus have the nasty surprise of coming home to find their eight-year-old engrossed in a rerun of *Texas Chainsaw Massacre Part 5*. How are they to explain to children, whose distinction between what is real and what is imaginary is tenuous, to say the least, that what they have just been watching has all been made with a lot of special effects? And above all, that they are not supposed to do the same to their next-door neighbours, no matter how angry at them they may get? Aside from a major review of our TV programmes, an obvious though drastic solution would be for parents to mount a lock onto their TV set! And this still does not affect the issue of irresponsible adults watching the wrong programme at the wrong time...

2. When Alexander the Great conquered the whole of the Greek peninsula, he did not encounter any major opposition: the Greek city-states were independent from each other, when they were not actively involved in local feuds, so he had no trouble overcoming them. Hence the proverb: "United we stand, divided we fall." Indeed, it seems as if unity were the only means to survive any kind of adversity. Since many politicians and rulers are aware of this, they actively encourage any kind of dissension among the ranks of their opponents. Unity would pose a threat, so it is all the more desirable to splinter the opposition. Conversely, any kind of group has to be aware of this when they launch into action: your opponents will be all too ready to sow the seeds of division and any kind of schism should be nipped in the bud. This may account for the drastic purges that have occurred regularly among political movements, while by no means making them more excusable: for the risk of unity at all costs is a certain ossification of the group, which eventually turns into a lifeless monolith. Surely there must be room for diversity within any kind of group, and unity should not be earned at the expense of the freedom of thought and expression of its members. This is nowhere truer than in a sports team: each player has to subordinate his style to the strategy of the whole team, but this does not mean he should turn into a lifeless zombie or lose any of his individual brilliance.

LANGUE VIVANTE II
LANGUE VIVANTE III

Barèmes

	L.V. II	L.V. III
A. Compétence linguistique	35	40
B. Compréhension de l'écrit	35	35
C. Expression personnelle	30	25

SUJET

A. COMPÉTENCE LINGUISTIQUE

I. L'action désignée par le groupe verbal souligné s'est-elle oui ou non produite dans le passé?

	OUI	NON
1. It's about time you <u>bought</u> your wife a diamond.		
2. He <u>would sit</u> there for hours and refuse to say a word. She was desperate.		
3. He <u>might</u> well <u>be</u> too young for this job.		
4. <u>Had I known</u> the truth, I woudn't have trusted him.		
5. We'd rather they <u>didn't come</u> at all.		

II. Écrivez dans la parenthèse l'élément auquel le pronom ou l'adjectif souligné renvoie.

1. They say everybody should bring <u>their</u> dictionaries. (. . . . .)
2. Laura admired the ship and wondered why <u>she</u> was called "Mouse". (. . . . .)
3. She wondered who the person who had killed Jennifer was; <u>she</u> would be at the trial anyway. (. . . . .)
4. They said that if somebody used <u>their</u> parking-space, <u>they</u> would be reported. 1 (. . . . .) 2 (. . . . .)

III. Mettez les verbes entre parenthèses au temps et/ou à la forme qui conviennent.

"I remember (look) . . . . away again because the man (just/terrify) . . . . me. I (not/know) . . . . which was more frightening: (look) . . . . at him or (look) . . . . at the gun...

You (see) .... guns like that on television on the news but you (not expect) .... to have them (point) .... right at you!"

Woman's Own. Oct. 19, 1992.

IV. Transformez en utilisant l'amorce fournie.

1. I'm sorry you can't play the piano.
   I wish ....
2. Why do you smoke?
   I'd rather...
3. I'm sorry I deceived her.
   I wish ....
4. I last saw them a month ago.
   I haven't ....
5. I went to Ireland in 1983.
   It is ages ....

V. Remettez les mots dans l'ordre pour faire une phrase correcte sans oublier la ponctuation.

1. gorgeous/she/a/creature/just/was
   ....
2. my friend/jacket/is desperate/has been/stolen/whose
   ....
3. friends/I have/more/the/I am/happier/the
   ....
4. two/read/paragraphs/first/the
   ....
5. difficult/it/however/make it/is/we shall
   ....

B. COMPRÉHENSION D'UN TEXTE ÉCRIT

Richard carried his father's tea through into the living-room and put it on his lap. This was the time of day he dreaded most: his mother at work, Sharon out playing, himself and his father cooped up together, silent and ill-at-ease.

5 He got out his books and spread them over the table. He sat down, trying not to hear the steady chomp-chomp of his father's jaws, the disgusting way he swilled tea around an already-too-full mouth. He could feel the tension. He could feel how his father hated the books. He wasn't just indifferent to them, he wasn't neutral: he really hated them.

10 When he sat looking at the newspaper, as he sometimes did, his eyes did not move across the page. Richard had noticed this, but didn't know

what it meant. Bills, letters, all that sort of thing, his father passed over to his mother. It was as though anything that involved reading or writing was woman's work.

15 So it was always like this in the late afternoons.

John Scaife hardly knew how it had come about. He knew only that he hated the books which were almost instruments of torture to him, so keenly did he remember the humiliations of his school days. Once and once only had he dared to show interest and that was because the book

20 his son was reading seemed to be full of pictures.

'What's that you're looking at, son?'

'Nothing.'

'Well, it must be something.'

'It's nothing to do with school. It's from the library.' He stared at his

25 father, defensively. 'It's about birds.'

'Birds!'

'Yes.' Briefly he showed a picture of some long-legged, white bird in flight. 'That's a heron.'

'Not a lot of use that, round here.'

30 For there were no birds. Only sparrows and starlings. And seagulls of course.

'I like the pictures.'

'Ah, well.' John rustled his newspaper uneasily. 'Only birds I ever fancy are in here.' And he showed a picture of a woman with big

35 breasts, smouldering on page three.

As soon as he had done it he was cursing himself. He saw Richard flinch and look away. He was at that awkward stage of early puberty: wincing, hypersensitive, fastidious. It was the last thing he should have said. Crude. Unnecessary. Not even true. What he wanted was to meet

40 the boy on common ground: to share jokes and interests, to introduce him to the world of work, pub, football. But he couldn't do it. Of course the boy was too young, but that was the least of it. His feet were set on a different path.

Pat Borker, *Union Street* (1982).

I. Cochez la bonne réponse.

1. The son is
   a) a bookseller,
   b) a school boy,
   c) a librarian,
   d) a bookkeeper.

2. The father
   a) has a passion for books,
   b) resents his son's interest in books,
   c) is too busy to read,
   d) thinks books are for women.

3. The father and the son
   a) loathe each other,
   b) are indifferent to each other,
   c) fail to communicate,
   d) are jealous of each other.
4. a) The situation is unbearable to both the father and the son.
   b) The situation is painful to the son only.
   c) Only the father suffers from the tension.
   d) Neither the son nor the father really minds.

II. *Le texte peut être divisé en deux parties. Complétez la phrase par des mots du texte (un blanc = un mot) de façon à bien indiquer le point de vue de la narration.*

In the first part, the relationship between the father and the son is seen through the eyes of the . . . . , whereas in the second part, we are given the . . . . 's point of view.

III. 1. *Situez le dialogue qui se trouve dans la 2ᵉ partie en cochant la bonne réponse.*

   a) ANTÉRIEUR
   b) POSTÉRIEUR   au moment de la narration.

   2. *Écrivez le(s) mot(s) qui justifie(ent) votre réponse.*
. . . .

IV. *TRUE or FALSE: cochez la bonne réponse et "justifiez-la" par une citation tirée du texte. Les questions portent sur la fin du texte, de la ligne 21 à la ligne 43.*

	T	F
1. The father seems to reveal some kind of interest in his son's reading.	☐	☐
2. The father couldn't help making a "funny" pun.	☐	☐
3. The son reacted positively to his father's pun.	☐	☐
4. The father felt relieved after the conversation.	☐	☐
5. The father understood his son's reaction.	☐	☐
6. The father was persuaded that his son would change in the future.	☐	☐

V. Parmi les sentiments suivants, quels sont ceux qu'éprouve le père en présence du fils et/ou le fils en présence du père.
Mettez une croix dans la case correspondante et justifiez votre réponse dans la colonne suivante par une citation tirée du texte.

	sentiments du père		sentiments du fils	
pride				
embarrassment				
repulsion				
despair				
frustration				

VI. 1. Citez deux expressions qui expliquent la haine du père à l'égard de l'écrit.

. . . .

2. Citez trois mots qui résument l'univers du père.

. . . .

3. Justifiez les affirmations suivantes par une citation du texte.
The father...
is illiterate.

. . . .

regrets his brutish attitude towards his son.

. . . .

C. EXPRESSION PERSONNELLE

I. Production semi-guidée (100 à 150 mots).

The mother is *worried* about the tension at home. She talks about it to a friend at work.
Although she understands her son's feelings, she *wishes* he would make an effort to improve his relationship with his father.
Write what *she* says.

II. Production libre (200 à 250 mots).

Traitez l'un des deux sujets au choix. Entourez le numéro du sujet choisi.

1. What does the word "star" mean to you?

2. DO YOU PERSONALLY CONSIDER CLOTHES OR PEOPLE'S PHYSICAL APPEARANCE IMPORTANT? WHAT IS THE ATTITUDE OF TEENAGE TOWARDS SUCH MATERIAL DETAILS?

2. Do you personally consider clothes or people's physical appearance important? What is the attitude of teenagers today towards such material details?

CORRIGÉS

A. COMPÉTENCE LINGUISTIQUE

I

1. non.
2. oui.
3. non.
4. non.
5. non.

II

1. everybody
2. the ship.
3. She (1er sujet).
4. 1. they (1er sujet).   2. somebody.

III

looking
just terrified
~~don't know~~ *didn't know*
looking
looking
see
don't expect
pointed

IV

1. I wish ~~I~~ *you* could play the piano.
2. I'd rather you didn't smoke.
3. I wish I hadn't deceived her.

4. I haven't seen them for a month.
5. It is ages since I last went to Ireland.

V

1. She was just a gorgeous creature.
2. My friend whose jacket has been stolen is desperate.
3. The more friends I have, the happier I am.
4. Read the first two paragraphs.
5. However difficult it is, we shall make it.

B. COMPRÉHENSION D'UN TEXTE ÉCRIT

I

1. b) a schoolboy.
2. b) resents his son's interest in books.
3. c) fail to communicate.
4. a) The situation is unbearable to both the father and the son.

II

1. son.
2. father.

III

1. a) ANTÉRIEUR au moment de la narration.
2. "Once and once only had he dared..."

IV

1. TRUE
   "What's that you're reading, son?"
2. TRUE
   "Only birds (=girls) I ever fancy are in here".
3. FALSE
   "He saw Richard flinch and look away".
4. FALSE
   "It was the last thing he should have said".
5. TRUE
   "He (=Richard) was at <u>that</u> (=the father was aware of it) stage of early puberty."

6. FALSE

"His (=Richard's) feet were set on a different path (from his father's).

V

Sentiments du père :
- pride: "...so keenly did he remember the humiliations of his school days."
- embarrassment: "As soon as he had done it he cursed himself".
- despair: "His (=Richard's) feet were set on a different path."
- frustration: "What he wanted most was to meet the boy on common ground. [...] But he couldn't do it."

Sentiments du fils :
- embarrassment: "...cooped up together, silent and ill-at-ease".
- repulsion: "...the disgusting way he (his father) swilled tea around".

VI

1. "...the books which were almost instruments of torture to him".
   "...so keenly did he remember the humiliations from his school days".
2. work, pub, football.
3. a) "When he sat <u>looking at</u> the newspaper, as he sometimes did, <u>his eyes did not move across the page</u>".
   "Bills, letters, all that sort of thing, his father passed over to his mother".   *was cursing*
   b) "As soon he had done it he ~~cursed~~ himself".
   "It was the last thing he should have said. Crude. Unnecessary. Not even true".

C. EXPRESSION PERSONNELLE

I. Expression semi-guidée

Madge, I worry about our Richard. He's always reading books and John feels he's trying to put him down for having left school when he was just twelve. They hardly ever talk to each other these days, I know John feels hurt but he can't help it. And Richard's not helping much: never a kind word for his father, you should see the looks he gives him at the dinner table. I know he's a sensitive child and his father often says the wrong thing, but I do wish he'd make an effort to communicate more. Why does he have to spread all his books all over the dining-room table when he knows his father doesn't like it? I know it can't be easy for him, but he could try going along to a football match, John would be so happy if he did.

II. Expression libre

1. What with the development of mass media in the modern world, we are swamped with would-be stars pouting at us from the front pages of magazines. I for one can't believe anyone seriously cares about next week's sub-Vanessa Paradis or Patrick Bruel. Yet I do believe the word "star" once had a meaning; while being no fan of fifties screen gods such as Marilyn Monroe or James Dean, I still feel they held something more special than our latter-day matinee idols. A star in those days was someone mysterious and unapproachable, someone millions of people fantasized about without a chance of ever meeting them. Our modern idols are all too willing to turn up on every chat show and have their private lives laid bare in the gutter press. Then again, maybe it was the same for those stars of the past and I'm idealizing them out of retrospective illusion. Still, I cannot help feeling there was more to them than that. They were surrounded by a special mystique and drove around in dark-windowed limousines; you only knew they lived in some fantastic mansion out in Beverly Hills; they often came to a tragic end, at which point a well-intentioned biographer could reveal to the gaping world all their inner turmoil, suffering and drug addictions. Many stars also aged gracefully, like Audrey Hepburn or Cary Grant, while losing none of their original appeal. Maybe there is no room left for any genuine star in the modern world. Or maybe I will only recognize them as stars once they have been laid to rest, utterly unapproachable at last!

2. No matter how much I may revile superficiality, I must admit I partly judge people on the clothes they wear. This may sound horribly cynical, but let me explain my meaning: I do not look at somebody in order to assess how much their clothes or haircut may have cost, but I definitely get a general idea of the kind of image the person is trying to project, which may or may not appeal to me. On the other hand, I try not to pass a definitive judgement on anybody before I have actually had a chance to talk to them. Strangely enough after what I said earlier, one kind of person that definitely puts me off is the type who will judge others on the clothes they wear! I feel teenagers nowadays lay far too much emphasis on brand names, for example; some people will simply not talk to you if you are wearing the wrong kind of jeans or shoes. Despite all the talk about equality and the right to be different, I still find most French teenagers amazingly conventional. This was brought home to me when I went on a school trip to England: the teenagers there all looked so different from each other and they were so much more extreme about it, I felt as if we French youths were carbon copies of each other. The other funny thing was that you could see very different-looking people talking to each other: an old English lady would not be frightened of speaking to a leather-clad punk, which would be just about unthinkable over here. All in all, I wish people would not stop at such material details when they meet someone.

SUJET

A. COMPÉTENCE LINGUISTIQUE

I. Accentuation

Entourez la syllabe qui porte l'accent principal :

1. ad ver ti sing   2. cri ti cism   3. po ver ty
4. spe ci fic   5. e co no my   6. e co no mic
7. in for ma tion   8. spe cia lized.

II. Complétez les phrases avec les prépositions qui conviennent si cela est nécessaire. Sinon écrivez Ø dans l'espace prévu.

1. JANE   : "Bill, are you coming with us tonight ?"
   BILL   : "I don't know. It depends . . . . the weather."

2. AL   : "Why does Mr Drake look so worried ?"
   HELEN : "He feels he is responsible . . . . the accident."

3. The suspect has been charged . . . . murder.

4. Do you think a child should always obey . . . . his parents ?

5. I am not surprised the boy threw a stone . . . . the dog. He is so aggressive !

6. The child refused to answer . . . . the policeman's questions.

III. Complétez cet extrait adapté d'un article de presse en utilisant les articles "the", "a", "an". Si l'article n'est pas nécessaire, écrivez Ø dans l'espace prévu.

Bill Clinton, ... American president-elect, has made . . . .
. . . . . powerful attack on . . . . activities of . . . . security
forces in Northern Ireland. In . . . . official letter to . . . .
prominent Irish-American, he calls for . . . . British government to
introduce . . . . more effective safeguards against . . . .
"use of lethal force" by . . . . army and . . . . police.

IV. *Construisez des phrases cohérentes en prenant des éléments dans la colonne II et en les reliant aux éléments de la colonne I à l'aide des mots de liaison se trouvant dans la liste ci-dessous ; tous les mots doivent être utilisés.*

Whereas / so that / while / unless / provided

I	II
1. Leave early	you are in Paris
2. You can't drive a car	you don't ride recklessly
3. You should pay him a visit	you won't miss the train
4. I enjoy meeting people	you have an insurance policy
5. I will lend you my bike	you hate being in a crowd

1. . . . .
2. . . . .
3. . . . .
4. . . . .
5. . . . .

V. *Récrivez les phrases suivantes sans en changer le sens en utilisant les amorces données :*

1. Mary doesn't behave like an adult.
   It's high time . . . .

2. Please, stop talking.
   I wish . . . .

3. The man was so friendly !
   You have no idea . . . .

4. People say Scottish castles are haunted.
   Scottish castles . . . .

5. I'm sure Peter is living in Tokyo now.
   Peter . . . .

6. Why didn't you tell her before ?
   You should. . . . .

7. We were surprised when we heard they had left for Italy.
   We didn't expect . . . .

8. This car is so expensive !
   What . . . .

9. It is three years since I last saw her.
   I. . . . .

10. If you go to bed early, you sleep better.
    The . . . . *, the* . . . .

VI. Mettez le verbe au temps et à la forme qui conviennent.

1. "........................... "Dracula yet?" (see/you)

2. "Yes, I........................... it yesterday." (see)

3. Richard .... his homework for two hours now, and he still hasn't finished. (do)

4. Mary will give you a ring when she ....
   (arrive)

5. If I'd know it was going to rain, I .... my umbrella. (take)

B. COMPRÉHENSION D'UN TEXTE ÉCRIT

The Queen winced as Jack Barker ground his cigarette out on the silk rug. A faint smell of burning rose between them. Jack fought the urge to apologise. The Queen stared at Jack disdainfully. His stomach gurgled. Her picture had hung in his classroom when he was struggling to learn
5   his nine times tables. In his boyhood he used to look to the Queen for inspiration. Prince Charles bent down and picked up the cigarette stub. He looked for somewhere to put it, but, finding nowhere suitable, he slipped it into his pocket.
Princess Margaret said, "Lilibet I've *got* to have a fag. Please!"
10   "May we open the windows, Mr Barker?" asked the Queen. Her accent cut into Jack like crystal. He half expected to bleed.
"No chance," he replied.
"Am I to have a house of my own, Mr Barker, or must I share with my daughter and son-in-law?" The Queen Mother gave Jack her famous
15   smile, but her hands were twisting the full skirt of her periwinckle dress into a knot.
"You'll get a pensioner's bungalow. It's your entitlement as an ordinary citizen of this country."
"A bungalow, good. I couldn't manage stairs. Will my staff be living
20   in or out?"
Jack laughed and looked at his fellow Republicans. Six men and six women, hand-picked to witness this historic occasion. They laughed along with Jack.
"You don't seem to understand. There'll be no staff, no dressers, no
25   cooks, secretaries, cleaners, chauffeurs."
Turning to the Queen he said, "You'll have to nip in now and then, help your mum out. But she'll probably be entitled to Meals on Wheels."
The Queen Mother looked quite pleased to hear this. "So I shan't
30   starve?"
"Under the People's Republican Party's rule, nobody in Britain will starve," said Jack.
Prince Charles cleared his throat and said, "Er, may one, er, enquire as to where? That is, the location...?"

35 "If you're asking me where you're all going, I'm not telling you. All I
    can say at the moment is that you'll all be in the same street, but you'll
    have strangers as next-door neighbours, working-class people. Here's a
    list of what you can take with you."
    Jack held out photocopies of each of the lists his wife had compiled
40 only two hours before. The lists were headed: *Essential Items;*
    Furniture; Fittings, suitable for two-bedroomed council house and pen-
    sioner's bungalow. The Queen Mother's list was much shorter, she
    noticed. Jack held the papers out, but nobody came forward to take
    them. Jack didn't move. He knew that one of them would crack.
45 Eventually Diana got up, she hated scenes. She took the papers from
    Jack and gave each member of the Royal Family their list. There was
    quiet for a few moments while they read. Jack fiddled with the gun in
    his pocket. Only he knew that it wasn't loaded.

"The Queen and I", 1992. Sue Townsend.

● **Compréhension globale**

Circle the letter corresponding to the right answer.

1. This text is
   a) a newspaper article.
   b) an extract from a history book.
   c) a passage from a romantic novel.
   d) a piece of political fiction.

2. The characters are
   a) at a political meeting.
   b) having a tea-party.
   c) discussing the advantages of the British Monarchy.
   d) having a confrontation.

3. How many generations of royals are present?

4. How many characters are present?

● **Compréhension détaillée**

*I. Say whether the following statements are right or wrong. Circle R or W
after each statement.*
*Justify your answer with a **short** quotation.*

1. Jack apologized to the Queen.   R - W
   . . . .

2. Jack had always been indifferent to the Queen.   R - W
   . . . .

3. Princess Margaret doesn't smoke.   R - W
   . . . .

4. The Queen Mother was not displeased about what she was
   being offered.   R - W
   . . . .

5. The Queen Mother will be allowed to employ a daily help.   R - W
....

6. The Queen Mother will have to cook all her meals.   R - W
....

7. Prince Charles was not interested in where their new home
   would be.   R - W
....

8. There will be only members and friends of the Royal Family
   in the street where they will live.   R - W
....

9. Jack was confident he would gain the upper hand in the end.   R - W
....

10. Jack had no intention of physically harming the Royal Family.   R - W
....

II. *Quote short phrases to illustrate the following statements.*

1. The UK has been turned into a republic of the communist type. (1 quotation)
....

2. Jack didn't feel completely at ease in his role. (3 quotations)
....
....
....

3. The Queen disapproved of Jack's provocative behaviour. (2 quotations)
....
....

4. Jack used familiar language to address the Royals. (1 quotation)
....

III. *Which title is the most appropriate ?*

Circle the letter corresponding to the right answer.
   a) The Royal Family is moving to a new palace.
   b) The Labour Party is taking over.
   c) The overthrow of the Bristish Monarchy.
   d) The end of Charles and Diana's marriage.

C. EXPRESSION PERSONNELLE

I. *Production semi-guidée (100 à 150 mots).*

Imagine the conversation between Queen Elizabeth and Prince Philip that evening. They express their feelings:
   – fury
   – relief or regret.
They also make plans for the future.

Traiter l'un des 2 sujets au choix.

1. As the saying goes:
   "There is no place like home." What is home to you? What would you like it to be?

2. There is growing dissatisfaction with the British Royal Family. However many remain strongly attached to this institution. What's your opinion on the subject?

CORRIGÉS

A. COMPÉTENCE LINGUISTIQUE

I

1. advertising.
2. criticism.
3. poverty.
4. specific.
5. economy.
6. economic.
7. information.
8. specialized.

II

1. on.   2. for.   3. with.   4. Ø.   5. at.   6. Ø.

III

Bill Clinton, the American president-elect, has made a powerful attack on the activities of the security forces in Northern Ireland. In an official letter to a prominent Irish-American, he calls for the British government to introduce more effective safeguards against the "use of lethal force" by the army and the police.

IV

1. Leave early so that you won't miss your train.
2. You can't drive a car unless you have an insurance policy.
3. You should pay him a visit while you are in Paris.
4. I enjoy meeting people whereas you hate being in a crowd.
5. I will lend you my bike provided you don't ride recklessly.

V

1. It's high time Mary started behaving like an adult.
2. I wish you would stop talking.
3. You have no idea how friendly the man was.
4. Scottish castles are said to be haunted.
5. Peter must be living in Tokyo now.
6. You should have told her before.
7. We didn't expect them to leave for Italy.
8. What an expensive car!
9. I haven't seen her for three years.
10. The earlier you go to bed, the better you sleep.

VI

1. Have you seen.
2. saw.
3. has been doing.
4. arrives.
5. would have taken.

B. COMPRÉHENSION D'UN TEXTE ÉCRIT

● Compréhension globale

1. d) a piece of political fiction.
2. d) having a confrontation.
3. Three.
4. Eighteen (18). In order of appearance: the Queen, Jack Barker, Prince Charles, Princess Margaret, the Queen Mother, twelve Republicans (six men and six women), Princess Diana.

● Compréhension détaillée

I

1. WRONG
   Jack fought the urge to apologize (=he didn't).
2. WRONG
   In his boyhood he used to look to the Queen for inspiration.
3. WRONG
   "Lilibet, I've *got* to have a fag (=cigarette). Please!"
4. RIGHT
   "A bungalow, good [...]."
5. WRONG
   "There'll be no staff [...]."
6. WRONG
   "She'll probably be entitled to Meals on Wheels."

7 WRONG
   "Er, may one, er, inquire as to where...? That is, the location...?"
8. WRONG
   "[...] you'll have strangers as next-door neighbours [...]"
9. RIGHT
   Jack didn't move. He knew that one of them would crack.
10. RIGHT
   Only he knew that it (= the gun in his pocket) wasn't loaded.

II

1. "Under the People's Republican Party's rule, nobody in Britain will starve."
2. a) Jack fought <u>the urge</u> to apologize.
   b) <u>Her accent cut into Jack</u> like crystal.
   c) Jack <u>fiddled</u> with the gun in his pocket.
3. a) The Queen winced [...].
   b) The Queen stared at Jack disdainfully.
4. "No chance".
   "nip in".
   "help your mum out".

II

c) The overthrow of the British monarchy.

C. EXPRESSION PERSONNELLE

I. Expression semi-guidée

QE = Queen Elizabeth   PP = Prince Philip
QE: I cannot believe this is happening!
PP: Do you realize, my dear, that we are being thrown out of our ancestral home? This is simply insufferable.
QE: What about my corgis? Who will look after them while we are away?
PP: Er... I'm afraid... to tell you the truth, I had the palace vet put them to sleep an hour ago, I thought it might be better for them. They would never have adjusted.
QE: You didn't! And what about our china? I am perfectly certain the rabble will smash it. Mother will be heartbroken.
PP: Speaking of which, I must confess I am not too sorry we shall have a place of our own at last. You know how sensitive you are around the old girl. We might even have a second honeymoon.

QE: Do you really mean that?

PP: Actually, I have even succeeded in getting a couple of tickets to the Bahamas without the usurpers finding out about it.

QE: Spiffing, Philip!

II. Expression libre

1. I am very tempted to echo the saying in the subject with a Hispanic proverb: "Home is the dust under the soles of my shoes." As far as I'm concerned, any place could be home to me, precisely as long as I felt at home there. While I feel no particular urge to move right yet, I wouldn't mind having the opportunity to relocate somewhere else. What matters most to me is to feel surrounded by people I love, and I'm sure this could happen just about anywhere. I do not mean by this that I'm not attached to people, quite the opposite in fact: what I don't want to feel bound by is the mass of material possessions that we all tend to hoard and which eventually trap us. This is why I can hardly imagine myself ever buying a house, because I would be afraid it might restrict my mobility. On the other hand, there are a number of things which I know I would require in order to feel completely at home: certain books and records, certain photographs, and of course certain people. Beyond that, I need sunshine and quiet, and maybe a cat. Then I could truly say: "there is no place like home", and I would be glad to come home every night. But if I ever felt I were giving more attention to the place than to people themselves, I might start to worry about myself. I might even move! Anyway, I am quite happy with my current home although I know I will be leaving it soon. I only hope I can recreate a home as nice as the one I grew up in.

2. Not being a Bristish citizen myself, I barely feel entitled to voice my opinion about the Bristish Royal Family. However, I must confess that I find them vaguely preposterous. All they ever seem to do these days is provide the British tabloids with their latest matrimonial antics, hardly my kind of reading material. If many people remain attached to them, it is more out of a sense of tradition and because, so the argument goes, the Royals embody the British national identity. Is Britain so desperately in need of an emblem that it can afford to sponsor such expensive figureheads? We should not forget that the Royal Family derive a comfortable income from their position, which seems quite out of pace with the current recession. Moreover, they are one of the wealthiest if not the wealthiest family in the kingdom. Do they really need to levy taxes in order to supplement their income?

On the other hand, it seems quite difficult to do away with them. There certainly seems no point in dethroning them and turning Britain into a republic. However, it would be only fair to reduce their income in keeping with the current state of British economy. As for the growing dissatisfaction with them, which may be nothing more than news fodder for Fleet Street, it may stem from their latest family troubles. Isn't the British public enlightened enough to realize that their Royals are only human beings, and that while they reign but may not rule the country, they have a right to be ruled by passions like anybody else?

SUJET

A. COMPÉTENCE LINGUISTIQUE

I. Le texte suivant est à compléter : quand un verbe est fourni, vous le mettrez au temps qui convient ou à la forme voulue, sinon vous proposez UN mot pour chaque blanc. Si vous estimez ne rien devoir écrire, mettez le signe ∅.

Last summer Dickie Jones and his wife spent their holidays in the Bahamas. One morning, just as they (1) .... (GET) ready to go to the beach, they received an urgent phone-call (2) .... the British police, informing them that their son, Michael, had been seriously (3) .... in a car crash and that he might die. They (4) .... their cases as quickly as possible and took the first plane home. During the (5) .... they talked about their son.

'We (6) .... never have agreed to leave Michael by (7) .... said Mrs Jones. 'Why didn't we make him (8) .... (COME) with us ? '

'He's 17 years old.' answered her husband. 'He isn't interested (9) .... (10) .... (SPEND) his holidays with us. Very (11) .... teenagers want to go on holiday with their parents these days.

'But if he'd come to the Bahamas with us, he (12) .... (HAVE) an accident,' sobbed his wife.

'You can't be sure of that,' said Dickie, trying to console her. 'He (13) .... have had an accident in the Bahamas. We aren't responsible (14) .... what happened.'

'I wonder how he is. The police didn't give us (15) .... information. They just said the accident was serious.'

When the plane landed (16) .... Heathrow Airport, they took a taxi (17) .... the hospital.

'I've got (18) .... good news for you,' said the doctor. 'Your son is much better.'

II. Complétez les phrases suivantes à l'aide d'un mot de liaison pris dans cette liste :

so that / in order to / in case / whereas / although / unless / despite.

1. The club rules forbid members to use the tennis courts .... they are wearing tennis shoes.
2. We closed the kitchen door .... the smell of fish wouldn't reach the living-room.
3. We always took some sandwiches when we left for a long walk .... we felt hungry.
4. John invited the Wilsons to his birthday party .... he couldn't stand them.
5. The Smiths usually spend their summer holidays abroad .... the Browns prefer to visit Britain.

III. Prendre un élément dans la première colonne et le relier, à l'aide d'un relatif à un élément de la deuxième colonne, afin d'obtenir quatre phrases. Écrivez les phrases ci-dessous :

He was furious when his car,	looked friendly to give me some directions.
The immigrants	you are talking don't live here any more.
I asked a man	was brand new, broke down.
The people of	papers were in order were admitted at once.

1. ....
2. ....
3. ....
4. ....

IV. Complétez les phrases à l'aide d'auxiliaires (may - could - must, etc.) et mettre le verbe au temps et à la forme corrects.

1. It was your own fault that your results were bad. You .... (WORK) harder.
2. It was dangerous to drive so fast. You .... (HAVE) an accident.
3. I can manage without you. You .... (COME) if you are too busy.
4. My sister said she saw my husband yesterday but he is in Brazil. She .... (SEE) him. It was impossible.

B. COMPRÉHENSION D'UN TEXTE ÉCRIT

(...) She dialled her number.

Her mother's voice. Flat. At the sound of it affection filled Alice, and she thought, I'll ask if she wants me to do some shopping for her on the way.

'Hello, Mum, this is Alice.'

5   Silence.

'It's Alice.'

A pause. 'What do you want?' The flat voice, toneless.

Alice, all warm need to overcome obstacles on behalf of everyone, said, 'Mum, I want to talk to you. You see, there's this house. I could
10   get the Council to let us stay on a controlled squat basis[1], you know, like Manchester? But we need someone to guarantee the electricity and gas.'

She heard a mutter, inaudible, then, 'I don't believe it!'

'Mum. Look, it's only your signature we want. We would pay it.'

A silence, a sigh, or a gasp, then the line went dead.

15   Alice, now radiant with a clear hot anger, dialled again. She stood listening to the steady buzz-buzz, imagining the kitchen where it was ringing, the great warm kitchen, the tall windows, sparkling (she had cleaned them last week, with such pleasure), and the long table where, she was sure, her mother was sitting now, listening to the telephone ring.
20   After about three minutes, her mother did lift the receiver and said, 'Alice, I know it is no use my saying this. But I shall say it. Again. I have to leave here. Do you understand? Your father won't pay the bills any longer. I can't afford to live here. I'll have trouble paying my own bills. Do you understand, Alice?'

25   'But you have all those rich friends.' Another silence. Alice then, in a full, maternal, kindly, lecturing voice, began, 'Mum, why aren't you like us? We *share* what we have. We help each other out when we're in trouble. Don't you see that your world is finished? The day of the rich selfish bourgeoisie is over. You are doomed...'

30   'I don't doubt it,' said Alice's mother, and Alice warmed into the purest affection again, for the familiar comforting note of irony was back in her mother's voice, the awful deadness and emptiness gone. 'But you have at some point to understand that your father is not prepared any longer to share his ill-gotten gains[2] with Jasper and all his
35   friends.'

'Well, at least he is prepared to see they are ill-gotten,' said Alice earnestly.

A sigh, 'Go away, Alice,' said Alice's mother. 'Just go away. I don't want to see you. I don't want to hear from you. Try to understand that
40   you can't say the things to people you said to me this morning and then just turn up, as if nothing had happened, with a bright smile, for another hand-out[3].'

The line went dead.

The Good Terrorist, Doris Lessing.

---

1. on a controlled squat basis: without paying any rent.
2. his ill-gotten gains: the money he made immorally.
3. hand-out: (here) financial help.

- **Compréhension globale**

I. Entourer la lettre a, b, ou c correspondant à l'affirmation correcte.

1. The text relates
   a) an argument over the phone.
   b) an interview.
   c) a friendly conversation.

2. The people involved are
   a) a father and his daughter Alice.
   b) a husband and his wife Alice.
   c) a mother and her daughter Alice.

3. The general tone of the conversation is
   a) relaxed and affectionate.
   b) uneasy and tense.
   c) matter-of-fact and casual.

4. At the end of the passage we can conclude that
   a) somebody has died.
   b) the conversation leads nowhere.
   c) the speakers are reconciled.

II. Cocher la case RIGHT ou WRONG

1. The following characters are mentioned in the conversation:

	RIGHT	WRONG
a) Alice's father, Jasper		
b) Alice's friend, Jasper		
c) Alice's father		
d) Alice's brother		
e) Jasper's friends		

2.
	RIGHT	WRONG
a) Alice rang her mother to ask her if she had any shopping to do.		
b) Alice rang her mother to ask her a favour.		
c) Alice had a phone call from her mother about her bills.		
d) Alice wanted to move into a house.		
e) the mother's signature could guarantee the electricity and gas.		

- **Compréhension détaillée**

I. A qui renvoient les pronoms/adjectifs possessifs et pronoms personnels suivants ? Mettre une croix dans la bonne colonne.

	Alice	The mother
1.1 <u>she</u> (dialled)		
1.1 <u>her</u> (number)		
1.3 <u>she</u> (wants)		
1.3 (for) <u>her</u>		
1.12 <u>she</u> (heard)		
1.17 <u>she</u> (had cleaned)		
1.25 <u>you</u> (have)		
1.33 <u>you</u> (have . . . . . to understand)		

II. Répondre en portant une croix dans la bonne colonne, et justifier ce choix en citant dans son intégralité un élément pertinent du texte. Indiquer la ligne.

	RIGHT	WRONG
1. On hearing what Alice wanted from her, her mother hung up. l..		
2. Alice expected her mother to pay her gas and electricity bills. l..		
3. Alice's mother was in the kitchen during the phone conversation. l..		
4. Alice had not been to her mother's for months. l..		
5. Alice's mother had money problems herself. l..		
6. Alice believed in solidarity. l..		
7. Alice's parents belonged to the working-class. l..		
8. This was the first time Alice had asked her mother for help. l..		

III. Trouver dans le texte des mots ou expressions équivalents à :

1. (l.1-11) to solve everybody's problems.

....

2. (l.15-22) her mother eventually answered the phone.

....

3. (l.15-22) I know I won't convince you.

....

4. (l.25-29) there is no future for you and your kind.

....

5. (l.30-35) reassuring.

....

6. (l.36-43) arrive unexpectedly and ask for more money.

....

IV. Parmi les réactions et les traits de caractère suivants notez par une croix s'ils s'appliquent à Alice, ou sa mère, ou aux deux.

	Alice		her mother	
	yes	no	yes	no
a) idealism				
b) exasperation				
c) resignation				
d) enthusiasm				
e) coldness				
f) sarcasm				
g) naivety				
h) effrontery				

V. Relire attentivement le texte et choisir pour chaque passage la réponse qui convient. Entourer a, b, ou c.

1. In the passage *from line 1 to 7,* we understand that
   a) Alice's mother sometimes forgot to do the shopping.
   b) Alice often did the shopping for her mother.
   c) Alice was convinced that her mother would invite her to come and visit her.

2. In the passage *from line 4 to 14,* we understand that
   a) Alice's mother took a long time recognising who was calling.
   b) Alice's mother thought her daughter only called when she wanted something from her.
   c) Alice's mother was furious because she was unable to help her daughter financially.

3. In the passage *from line 25 to 29* we understand that
   a) Alice is suggesting it might be a solution for her mother to come and live with her.
   b) Alice would be ashamed if her mother had to beg her rich friends to help her.
   c) Alice had not given up the hope of converting her mother to her ideas.

4. In the passage *from line 30 to 37*, we understand that
   a) Alice's anger disappeared on hearing the irony in her mother's voice.
   b) Alice's anger disappeared on hearing that her father was going to change his way of life.
   c) Alice's anger disappeared when she realised that her mother finally agreed with her.

5. In the *last part of the text (line 38 to 43)*, we understand that
   a) Alice's mother couldn't stand Alice's condescending smiles any longer.
   b) Alice's mother didn't want Alice to visit her constantly.
   c) Alice's mother thought her daughter was a hopeless case.

C. EXPRESSION ÉCRITE

I. Production semi-guidée (100-150 mots).

Alice writes a letter to her father explaining why she does not approve of his way of life. Use expressions of indignation, disagreement, reproach.

II. Production libre (200-250 mots).

Le candidat traitera l'*un* des deux sujets *au choix* :
1. When you leave school, would you rather continue living with your parents or live on your own? Discuss the advantages and disadvantages of both.
2. Do you agree that 'the day of the rich, selfish bourgeoisie is over'?

CORRIGÉS

A. COMPÉTENCE LINGUISTIQUE

I

1. were getting.	7. himself.	13. might
2. from.	8. come.	14. for.
3. injured.	9. in.	15. any.
4. packed.	10. spending.	16. at.
5. flight.	11. few.	17. to.
6. should.	12. wouldn't have had.	18. some / Ø.

II

1. unless.
2. so that.
3. in case.
4. although.
5. whereas.

III

1. He was furious when his car, which was brand new, broke down.
2. The immigrants whose papers were in order were admitted at once.
3. I asked a man who looked friendly to give me some directions.
4. The people of whom you're talking don't live here any more.

IV

1. should have worked.
2. could have had.
3. needn't come / don't have to come.
4. can't have seen.

B. COMPRÉHENSION D'UN TEXTE ÉCRIT

● Compréhension globale

I

1. a) an argument over the phone.
2. c) a mother and her daughter Alice.
3. b) uneasy and tense.
4. b) the conversation leads nowhere.

II

1.
RIGHT: b) Alice's friend, Jasper,   c) Alice's father,
        e) Jasper's friends.
WRONG: a) Alice's father, Jasper   d) Alice's brother.
2.
RIGHT: b, d, e.
WRONG: a, c.

- **Compréhension détaillée**

I

<u>Alice</u>: she dialled; she heard; she had cleaned; you have to understand.
<u>The mother</u>: her number; she wants; for her; you have.

II

1. RIGHT
   [...] then the line went dead.
2. WRONG
   "Look, it's only your signature we want. We would pay it."
3. RIGHT
   [...] imagining the kitchen where it was ringing [...]
4. WRONG
   [...] she had cleaned them last week, with such pleasure [...]
5. RIGHT
   "I can't afford to live here. I'll have trouble paying my own bills.
6. RIGHT
   "We share what we have. We help each other out when we're in trouble."
7. WRONG
   "Don't you see that your world is finished? The day of the rich selfish bourgeoisie is over."
8. WRONG
   "[...] another handout".

III

1. to overcome obstacles on behalf of everyone.
2. her mother did lift the receiver.
3. I know it is no use my saying this.
4. You are doomed.
5. comforting.
6. turn up [...] for another handout.

IV

1. <u>Alice</u>: idealism, exasperation, enthusiasm, naivety, effrontery.
2. <u>Her mother</u>: exasperation, resignation, coldness, sarcasm.

V

1. c) Alice was convinced that her mother would invite her to come and visit her.
2. b) Alice's mother thought her daughter only called her when she wanted something from her.
3. c) Alice had not given up hope of converting her mother to her ideas.
4. a) Alice's anger disappeared on hearing the irony in her mother's voice.
5. c) Alice's mother thought her daughter was a hopeless case.

C. EXPRESSION PERSONNELLE

I. Expression semi-guidée

Dear Dad,
I can only say I'm shocked by the way you're treating Mum. What you do with your private life is your own business, but you have no right to turn her out on the street. Besides, the way you keep refusing to lend me money when you know I will pay it back is absolutely disgusting. Surely you have a few quid to spare with all the money you're making on the backs of your employees. And by the way, why didn't you answer my previous letter? Couldn't you afford the stamp or had you lost my address? This may be the way capitalists like you get richer, by pinching on every penny, but I have no intention of leading such a life of human misery. I am proud to inform you that I have just moved into a squat with a group of responsible, caring friends and we are going to get it registered. I hope I never have to ask for money from you again.

Alice.

II. Expression libre

1. When I leave school, I will most certainly have to live on my own as I have been accepted on a BTS course a long way from home and it would not be practical to commute every day. This is not really a matter of personal choice, but anyway, if it were entirely up to me, I still think I would rather leave home. I know it won't be easy to adjust to the loneliness at first, which is why I am thinking of sharing a flat

with two friends from high school who will be on the same course. Besides, I know I will miss my parents and my brother but at least I will be able to see them every weekend. I will probably also miss all sorts of funny things like homecooking (my parents are both great cooks!) and the feel of the house around me at night, but on the other hand this will be a great opportunity to spread my wings and develop my independence. I have older friends who waited until they were twenty-five before leaving home and they found it quite traumatic when it did happen. True, they enjoyed the safety of home for all those years and it must have made it easier for them to get on with their studies, but at the same time I can't help feeling that they missed out on something essential in their late teens and early twenties. Moreover, they found it all the more difficult to stand on their own two feet once they left home at last: they had always been pampered and it took them a long while to learn all the little tricks involved in living alone. Since you have to become an adult at some point, I would rather do it now to give myself time to get used to the idea!

2. When Alice claims that "the day of the rich, selfish bourgeoisie is over", we are given to understand that she is little more than a cartoon leftie. However, we may ask ourselves how seriously we should take this statement. What she probably means is that the rich, selfish upper class should be destroyed, or at least that it might as well gracefully withdraw from the social and economic scene to let new, more capable, obviously working-class hands take control of the country if not the whole world. To a large extent, it is true that most of the wealth of the planet still resides in a relatively small number of hands. However, it is hard to gauge how to transfer efficiently this wealth to new people or groups in command without running into a corrupt state-run economy. On the other hand, if we take this statement to mean simply that the rich, selfish bourgeoisie no longer is what it used to be, then it is hard to disagree: although there still are some remarkably rich families, their wealth is nothing compared to what it used to be fifty or a hundred years ago. Finally, maybe what Alice simply meant was that the days of selfish accumulation of wealth are over. In that sense again, she may be right: the modern bourgeoisie are probably not so much interested in the hoarding of wealth for its own sake as in the display of status symbols that bear witness to its social distinction. However, it is hard to be entirely optimistic about the final disappearance of greed in the make-up of mankind; after all only a minority can ever become true philosophers genuinely detached from wordly pursuits!

SUJET

A. COMPÉTENCE LINGUISTIQUE

I. Choose the correct answer.

1. He . . . . . . have done such a thing: it doesn't look like him!
   a) can't   b) mustn't   c) may not

2. Look at the camera he's got! He . . . . . . be a professional reporter.
   a) can   b) ought   c) must

3. They . . . . . . use their calculators; it's strictly forbidden.
   a) couldn't   b) mustn't   c) don't have to

4. You . . . . . . hurry, we can wait.
   a) had better   b) mustn't   c) needn't

5. I haven't seen him lately: he . . . . . . be on holiday.
   a) may   b) should   c) can't

6. How . . . . . . he do such an awful thing? That was a nasty trick indeed!
   a) should   b) can   c) could

II. Put the verbs into the correct forms and tenses

"I (1. to remember) the night Kennedy (2. to be assassinated)", says Peter Eagle; "it is an event which (3. to remain) engraved in my mind ever since. I was fifteen at the time, and at boarding school. I (4. to come back) from the gym when my friend Snoo yelled out of the window: "Kennedy (5. to be assassinated)". I couldn't believe it. I (6. to feel) a lump in my throat. That evening, everyone in the boarding-house was quiet. We did our homework, but everyone (7. to think) of what (8. to happen) that day."

III. Turn the following dialogue into reported speech.

BOB: "Did you see Mary last week?"
JEREMY: "No, I didn't; I'll ring her tomorrow."
BOB: "Tell her to remember our appointment on Friday if you can reach her."

IV. Match the following sentences.

1. She'll be late unless
2. He usually works overtime whereas
3. She's sure to catch her plane provided
4. She's already missed the plane several times though

a) she doesn't leave home too late.
b) she always take care to leave home early enough to avoid traffic jam.
c) she leaves at once.
d) she always leaves as soon as work is over.

V. Reorder the following words in order to get meaningful sentences.

1. did - wanted - she - what - do - to - say - she - ? -
2. ; - goes - I - church - don't - regularly - she - to - . -
3. , - he - he - however - his - birthday - thoughtful - has forgotten - 's - wife - is - . -

VI. Using the prompts given, rewrite the following sentences without changing the meaning.

1. You ought to change your sweat-shirt, it's so dirty ! Why . . . .
2. It's probably going to rain this afternoon; it's very cloudy indeed ! It's . . . .
3. This is the most exciting book I've ever read ! I've . . . .
4. There are many TV channels now; as a consequence people go to the cinema less and less. The more . . . . . .
5. Someone called him from the office just after he had left. No sooner . . . . .

B. COMPRÉHENSION D'UN TEXTE ÉCRIT

[...] As he moved he heard footfalls in the street, the sound of several men walking rapidly. Charlie Stowe was old enough to feel surprise that anybody was about. The footsteps came nearer, stopped; a key was turned in the shop door, a voice said : "Let him in," and then he heard his
5 father, "If you wouldn't mind being quiet, gentlemen. I don't want to wake up the family." There was a note unfamiliar to Charlie in the · undecided voice. A torch flashed and the electric globe burst into blue light. The boy held his breath; he wondered whether his father would hear his heart beating, and he clutched his night-shirt tightly and prayed,
10 "O God, don't let me be caught." Through a crack in the counter he could see his father where he stood, one hand held to his stiff collar, between two men in bowler hats and belted mackintoshes. They were strangers.

"Have a cigarette," his father said in a voice dry as a biscuit. One of
15 the men shook his head. "It wouldn't do, not when we are on duty.
Thank you all the same." He spoke gently, but without kindness:
Charlie Stowe thought his father must be ill. "Mind if I put a few in my
pocket?" Mr. Stowe asked, and when the man nodded he lifted a pile of
Gold Flake and Players from a shelf and caressed the packets with the
20 tips of his fingers.

"Well," he said, "there's nothing to be done about it, and I may as
well have my smokes." For a moment Charlie feared discovery, his
father stared round the shop so thoroughly; he might have been seeing it
for the first time. "It's a good little business," he said, "for those that
25 like it. The wife will sell out, I suppose. Else the neighbours'll be wrecking it. Well, you want to be off. A stitch in time. I'll get my coat."

"One of us'll come with you, if you don't mind," said the stranger
gently.

"You needn't trouble. It's on the peg here. There, I'm all ready."
30 [...] When the door had closed Charlie tiptoed upstairs and got into
bed. He wondered why his father had left the house again so late at night
and who the strangers were. Surprise and awe kept him for a little while
awake. It was as if a familiar photograph had stepped from the frame to
reproach him with neglect. He remembered how his father had held tight
35 to his collar, and he thought for the first time that, while his mother was
boisterous and kindly, his father was very like himself, doing things in
the dark which frightened him. It would have pleased him to go down to
his father and tell him that he loved him, but he could hear through the
window the quick steps going away. He was alone in the house with his
40 mother, and he fell asleep.

Graham Greene. *I Spy (adapted from)*.

● **Compréhension globale**

I. Choose the most appropriate title for the text.

   a) Stealing.
   b) Like father like son.
   c) Fight in the night.

II. Choose the correct answer and justify by quoting the text.

1. Charlie observed the whole scene
   a) from a hidden spot upstairs.
   b) from a hidden spot in the shop.
   c) through a crack in his bedroom floor.

2. Mr Stowe
   a) resigned himself to his fate and followed the men.
   b) decided not to follow the men before selling the shop.
   c) claimed his innocence but accepted to follow the men.

3. The end of the story
   a) unveiled the mystery surrounding Mr Stowe's going away.
   b) didn't bring any answer to Charlie's questions about his father.
   c) revealed the strangers' identity and the reason for their visit.

4. At the end, Charlie's opinion of his father
   a) stayed the same.
   b) changed for the better.
   c) changed for the worse.

5. Charlie realized
   a) his father and mother had the same tempers.
   b) his father and mother had different tempers.
   c) he had the same temper as his mother.

• Compréhension approfondie

I. Find out the equivalent of the underlined words.

1. The man nodded:
   a) the man forbade Mr Stowe to take a few packets of cigarettes.
   b) the man agreed to Mr Stowe's taking a few packets of cigarettes.
   c) the man objected to Mr Stowe's taking a few packets of cigarettes.

2. His father stared round the shop so thoroughly:
   a) intensely   b) suspiciously   c) angrily

3. Charlie tiptoed upstairs:
   a) he rushed upstairs as fast as he could.
   b) he walked back to his room as silently as he could.
   c) he crawled back to his room.

4. His mother was boisterous:
   a) discreet   b) cautious   c) lively.

II. Right of wrong ? Justify by quoting the text.

1. When he heard his father speak, Charlie felt immediately reassured.
2. When Mr Stowe and the men entered the shop, Charlie was about to go out for a walk.
3. Charlie felt quite safe where he was hiding.
4. Charlie had never seen the men before.
5. Mr Stowe was both polite and tense.
6. The men refused to have a cigarette out of politeness.
7. The men were rather brutal with Mr Stowe.
8. The men weren't too sure Mr Stowe wouldn't try to escape.
9. Charlie couldn't help feeling guilty after his father had left.
10. Charlie understood his father better at the end of the story.

III. Among the following words, choose four that correspond to Charlie's feelings throughout the text and for each, quote a passage to justify your choice.

surprise - excitement - joy - panic - pleasure - perplexity - satisfaction - regret - relief

IV. Find in the text sentences showing

1. how Charlie got aware that something was wrong with his father.
2. that Mr Stowe felt sorry that he should have to stop running his shop.
3. Mr. Stowe was convinced he'd never come back.

C. EXPRESSION PERSONNELLE

I. Expression semi-guidée (100-150 mots).

Imagine Charlie's thought as he is in his bed after his father has left: he expresses his anxiety, his doubts, his remorse, his wishes, etc.

II. Expression libre (200-250 mots).

Choose one of the following subjects:

1. Do you think it's always easy to communicate with the people we love best?
2. Imagine a continuation to the father's story.

CORRIGÉS

A. COMPÉTENCE LINGUISTIQUE

I

1. a) can't.
2. c) must.
3. b) mustn't.
4. c) needn't.
5. a) may.
6. c) could.

II

1. remember.
2. was assassinated.
3. has remained.

4. was coming.
5. has been assassinated.
6. felt.
7. was thinking.
8. had happened.

III

Bob asked Jeremy if he had seen Mary the week before. Jeremy replied he hadn't. He added that he would ring her the next day. Bob asked him to tell her to remember their appointment that Friday if he could reach her.

IV

1. She'll be late unless she leaves at once.
2. He usually works overtime whereas she always leaves as soon as work is over.
3. She's sure to catch her plane provided she doesn't leave home too late.
4. She's already missed the plane several times though she always takes care to leave home early enough to avoid traffic jams.

V

1. What did she say she wanted to do?
2. She goes to church regularly; I don't.
3. However thoughtful he is, he has forgotten his wife's birthday.

VI

1. Why don't you change your sweatshirt, it's so dirty!
2. It's so cloudy it's bound to rain this afternoon.
3. I've never read such an exciting book.
4. The more TV channels there are, the less people go to the cinema.
5. No sooner had he left than someone called him from the office.

B. COMPRÉHENSION D'UN TEXTE ÉCRIT

● **Compréhension globale**

I

b) Like father, like son.

II

1. b) from a hidden spot in the shop.
2. a) resigned himself to his fate and followed the men.
3. b) didn't bring any answer to Charlie's questions about his father.
4. b) changed for the better.
5. b) his father and mother had different tempers.

- **Compréhension approfondie**

I

1. b) the man agreed to Mr Stowe's taking a few packets of cigarettes.
2. a) intensely.
3. b) he walked back to his room as silently as he could.
4. c) lively.

II

1. WRONG
   There was a note unfamiliar to Charlie in the undecided voice.
2. WRONG
   [...] he clutched his nightshirt tightly [...]
3. WRONG
   [he] prayed: "O God, don't let me be caught."
4. RIGHT
   They were strangers.
5. RIGHT
   "Have a cigarette," his father said in a voice dry as a biscuit.
6. WRONG
   "It wouldn't do, not when we are on duty. [...]"
7. WRONG
   He spoke gently [...].
8. RIGHT
   "One of us'll come with you, if you don't mind," [...].
9. RIGHT
   It was as if a familiar photograph had stepped out of its frame to reproach him with neglect.
10. RIGHT
    [...] he thought for the first time that [...] his father was very like himself [...].

III

surprise:
Charlie Stowe was old enough to feel surprise [...].

panic:

[...] he clutched his nightshirt tightly and prayed: "O God, don't let me be caught [...]."

perplexity:

He wondered why his father had left the house again so late at night and who the strangers were.

regret:

It would have pleased him to go down to his father and tell him that he loved him, but he could hear through the window the quick steps going away.

IV

1. [...] his voice dry as a biscuit.
2. [he] caressed the packets with the tips of his fingers.
3. "Its a good little business," he said, "for those that like it. The wife will sell out, I suppose. [...]"

C. EXPRESSION PERSONNELLE

I. Expression semi-guidée

I wonder where Dad's gone, I hope those men don't hurt him. I wish I'd said something, maybe I should have gone with him. Why am I such a coward? I wish I were more like Dad, he didn't seem upset at all. Where are they taking him? I wonder who they were and what they wanted with him. They looked like those secret police agents you see in films or something. I hope Mum won't be too upset in the morning when she realizes he's gone. I shouldn't think about those things. He'll be back, I'm sure. He's never done anything wrong in his whole life, surely they won't keep him forever? But what if he never came back? That would be too terrible. I must stop thinking about it right now, and then he'll be back in the morning and everything's going to be all right.

II. Expression libre

1. Communication may seem easy, but communicating with someone you love very dearly can be one of the most difficult things in the world. It is so easy to have a fight with somebody you love simply because either of you said the wrong thing or misunderstood something the other had said. This may seem paradoxical: indeed, why shouldn't we be able to communicate freely with somebody we ought to feel particularly confident with? But love easily breeds distrust, or worse still, self-mistrust: you are afraid of showing your own feelings for fear of getting hurt, so you end up saying all the wrong things in order to disguise your feelings. Sometimes, just because you are afraid of losing the affection of someone you love, you will conceal your own affection, thereby running a risk of wrecking the relationship for good. Or you don't want to show that you are vulnerable (loving does make you vulnerable!) so you put on this big tough attitude and you only succeed in hurting the other person's feelings. Rilke was right when he said that loving someone else was surely the most difficult experience in the world, the one for which everything else was but a rehearsal. Fortunately, loving can also give you the strength to overcome your inhibitions and to make the effort to communicate in a genuine fashion, no matter how hard it may seem at first. Then love truly blooms into more than the chance encounter of two self-enclosed individuals, giving rise to something that transcends the subjective barriers of selfishness and fear.

2. The two men were walking silently on either side of Mr Stowe. He fumbled in his pocket for a cigarette, the man on his left glanced at him before offering a light. Mr Stowe inhaled deeply to conceal the rising anxiety in his chest. When they finally reached the black, unmarked car, he knew where they were taking him. He crushed the butt under his foot and climbed in, the man on his right took the wheel while the other sat next to him throughout the whole journey.
He asked in an expressionless voice: "When did you decide to call me back?"
The man next to him groaned. "Oh, a while ago. We were running out of agents and we made a random choice. Too bad it had to be you. Hope your family manage all right without you. The boss spoke very highly of your talents, you seem perfect for the mission."
"Have you got any clues as to... do you know what it'll consist of?"
The driver looked back in the rearview mirror.
"Sorry, old chap, but you'll have to wait till we get to the headquarters to ask that kind of question."
Mr Stowe sat back in the posh black leather seat, looking idly at the featureless hamlets the car was creeping through. He would find out soon enough, and besides, what did it matter now where they posted him? They could send him off to the moon for all he cared. He had been deluding himself for all those years, waiting for a call which he hoped would never come.

SUJET

A. COMPÉTENCE LINGUISTIQUE

I. *Complétez les phrases suivantes en mettant le verbe au temps et à la forme qui conviennent.*

1. He (to be punished) if he hadn't done his homework.
   . . . .

2. She's been playing the cello since she (to be) twelve.
   . . . .

3. The student (to pass) his exam if he had worked harder.
   . . . .

4. Our neighbour (just, to buy) a new car.
   . . . .

5. I bet you that I (to finish) this book before noon.
   . . . .

6. She (to talk) on the phone with her boy friend for two hours.
   . . . .

7. I (to work) since you left this morning. I need a break now.
   . . . .

8. When she opened her bag, she realized that she (not, to take) her purse.
   . . . .

9. They are late. They must (to stop) at the pub.
   . . . .

10. Is Betty at home ? No, she (to go) to the hairdresser's.
    . . . .

II. *Reformulez les énoncés suivants en utilisant les amorces proposées.*

1. I suggest we take a cab.
   How . . . .

2. We complained about the meal but in vain.
   It was no use . . . .
3. It's highly probable he said that on purpose.
   He . . . .
4. He will soon come to a decision.
   It won't be long . . . .
5. He can borrow my car, I don't object to it.
   I don't mind . . . .

III. Mettre au discours indirect.

1. "I'll do my best to help you," he told them.
   . . . .
2. "My mother must be wondering where I am," Jane said.
   . . . .
3. "Have you ever heard such nonsense?" she asked him.
   . . . .
4. "Don't answer back," she warned him.
   . . . .
5. "What will he say when he learns the truth?" she wondered.
   . . . .

IV. Mettre au passif.

1. They should have tested the blood before giving it to the patients.
   . . . .
2. The mechanic is going to test the car in a minute.
   . . . .
3. They are taking him to the police station.
   . . . .
4. His father told him not to take the car to go out with his friends.
   . . . .
5. People say that tea is better than coffee.
   . . . .

V. Complétez avec le "tag" qui convient.

1. That English test was very easy, ...
2. We should have a say in the matter, ...
3. There is nothing more to add, ...
4. You can't spread such lies about him, ...
5. People shouldn't drink and drive, ...

B. COMPRÉHENSION D'UN TEXTE ÉCRIT

Ida was very unhappy that she had kept Frank on when she could have got rid of him so easily. She was to blame and she actively worried. Though she had no evidence, she suspected Helen was interested in the clerk. Something was going on between them. She did not ask her
5 daughter what, because a denial would shame her. And though she had tried she felt she could not really trust Frank. Yes, he had helped the business, but how much would they have to pay for it? Sometimes when she came upon him alone in the store, his expression, she told herself, was sneaky. He sighed often, muttered to himself, and if he saw he was
10 observed, pretended he hadn't. Whatever he did there was more in it than he was doing. He was like a man with two minds. With one he was here, with the other some place else. Even while he read he was doing more than reading. And his silence spoke a language she couldn't understand. Something bothered him and Ida suspected it was her
15 daughter. Only when Helen happened to come into the store or the back while he was there, did he seem to relax, become one person. Ida was troubled, although she could not discover in Helen any response to him. Helen was quiet in his presence, detached, almost cold to the clerk. She gave him for his restless eyes nothing – her back. Yet for this reason,
20 too, Ida worried.

One night, after Helen had left the house, when her mother heard the clerk's footsteps going down the stairs, she quickly got into a coat, wrapped a shawl around her head and trudged through a sprinkle of snow after him. He walked to the movie house several blocks away, paid
25 his money, and passed in. Ida was almost certain that Helen was inside, waiting for him. She returned home with nails in her heart and found her daughter upstairs, ironing. Another night, she followed Helen to the library. Ida waited across the street, shivering for almost an hour in the cold, until Helen emerged, then followed her home. She chided herself
30 for her suspicions but they would not fly from her mind. Once, listening from the back, she heard her daughter and the clerk talking about a book. This annoyed her. And when Helen later happened to mention that Frank had plans to begin college in the autumn, Ida felt he was saying that only to get her interested in him.

Bernard Malamud, *The Assistant.*

• Compréhension globale

I. Circle the letter corresponding to the right answer.

1. The events take place in:
   a) spring   b) summer   c) autumn   d) winter
2. Frank is:
   a) a priest   b) a college student   c) a salesman

3. Ida is:
   a) a store owner   b) a saleswoman c) a customer
4. Ida's attitude towards Frank reflects:
   a) hatred   b) distrust   c) trust
5. Helen's attitude towards Frank reveals that she is:
   a) in love   b) indifferent   c) friendly`

- **Compréhension détaillée**

I. Circle RIGHT or WRONG, justify your answer by quoting from the text.

1. Ida wished she had asked Frank to stop working for her.   RIGHT - WRONG
   ....

2. Ida could read Frank's mind like an open book.   RIGHT - WRONG
   ....

3. Helen's behaviour showed that she was in love with Frank.   RIGHT - WRONG
   ....

4. Ida was worried because Helen seemed to conceal her true feelings towards Frank.   RIGHT - WRONG
   ....

5. Ida couldn't help thinking that Frank was to meet Helen at the movie house.   RIGHT - WRONG
   ....

6. Ida's suspicion was founded.   RIGHT - WRONG
   ....

7. Ida went with Helen to the library.   RIGHT - WRONG
   ....

8. Ida resented being so suspicious but couldn't help it.   RIGHT - WRONG
   ....

9. Frank was an efficient clerk.   RIGHT - WRONG
   ....

10. Frank didn't intend to remain a clerk all his life.   RIGHT - WRONG
    ....

II. Find equivalents for the following words and phrases in the text.

1. Ida decided to <u>go on employing</u> Frank.
2. There was no <u>proof</u> that Helen was in love.

3. She could never understand what he said because he <u>mumbled</u> all the time.

4. <u>He was worried about something</u>.

5. <u>Her heart was aching with pain and sadness</u>.

III. Translate into French

"Ida was very unhappy that she had kept Frank on when she could have got rid of him so easily. She was to blame and she actively worried. Though she had no evidence, she suspected Helen was interested in the clerk."

C. EXPRESSION PERSONNELLE

I. Production semi-guidée (about 150 words).

Unable to talk frankly to her daughter, Ida writes Helen a letter telling her why she distrusts Frank. She also tries to persuade Helen not to see Frank any more.

II. Production libre (about 200 words).

Traitez l'un des deux sujets suivants :

1. Is Ida's behaviour typical of normal maternal love ?
2. Can people coming from different social and ethnic backgrounds make successful marriages ?

CORRIGÉS

A. COMPÉTENCE LINGUISTIQUE

I

1. would have been.
2. was.
3. would have passed.
4. has just bought.

5. will have finished.
6. has been talking.
7. have been working.
8. had not taken.
9. have stopped.
10. has gone.

II

1. How about taking a cab?
2. It was no use complaining about the meal.
3. He must have said that on purpose.
4. It won't be long before he comes to a decision.
5. I don't mind his borrowing my car.

III

1. He told them he would do his best to help them.
2. Jane said her mother must be wondering where she was.
3. She asked him if he had ever heard such nonsense.
4. She warned him not to answer back.
5. She wondered what he would say when he learnt the truth.

IV

1. The blood should have been tested before being given to the patients.
2. The car is going to be tested in a minute.
3. He is being taken to the police station.
4. He was told not to take the car to go out with his friends.
5. Tea is said to be better than coffee.

V

1. wasn't it?
2. shouldn't we?
3. is there?
4. can you?
5. should they?

B. COMPRÉHENSION D'UN TEXTE ÉCRIT

● Compréhension globale

1. d) winter.
2. c) a salesman.

3. a) a store owner.
4. b) distrust.
5. b) indifferent (or a) in love, depending on whose point of view you adopt).

• Compréhension détaillée

I

1. RIGHT
   Ida was very unhappy that she had kept Frank on.
2. WRONG
   His silence spoke a language she could not understand.
3. WRONG
   Helen was very quiet in his presence, detached, almost cold to the clerk.
4. RIGHT
   Yes, for this reason too, Ida worried.
5. RIGHT
   Ida was almost certain that Helen was inside, waiting for him.
6. WRONG
   [She] found her daughter upstairs, ironing.
7. WRONG
   [...] she followed Helen to the library.
8. RIGHT
   She chided herself for her suspicions, but they wouldn't fly from her mind.
9. RIGHT
   Yes, he had helped the business.
10. RIGHT
    Frank had plans to begin college in the autumn.

II

1. keep on.
2. evidence.
3. muttered.
4. He was like a man with two minds.
5. [She had] nails in her heart.

III

Ida était très malheureuse d'avoir gardé Frank à son poste alors qu'il lui aurait été tellement facile de se débarrasser de lui. Elle s'en voulait et se faisait de gros soucis. Même sans aucune preuve, elle soupçonnait Helen de s'intéresser à l'employé.

C. EXPRESSION PERSONNELLE

I. Expression semi-guidée

Dear Helen,

I know it must seem strange for me to be writing a letter when we are living under the same roof, but this is about something I haven't been able to bring myself to tell you about. Lately I've been having rising doubts about Frank's honesty. Honesty isn't even the word I'm looking for, it's something both vague and threatening. I feel as if there were more to him than meets the eye, I have this nagging suspicion he's up to something unsavoury and though I know it's perfectly silly of me, I can't shake off these misgivings. I honestly wish you would stop seeing him, because God knows what this man may be capable of. You may be fonder of him than you care to admit, but will you please do this for me? I feel quite ashamed of myself for writing this letter, but this is the only way I could let you know. Remember I'm only doing this out of my love for you.

Mum

II. Expression libre

1. In my view, Ida is somewhat paranoid: she has got very little to pin her anxieties onto, yet she hangs on to her suspicions and goes so far as to stand in the cold and snow for almost an hour because she believes her daughter to be at risk. Worse still, the less conclusive evidence of Frank's (and Helen's) guilt she finds, the more convinced she becomes that they are having a secret affair right in front of her. Personally, I feel that a truly loving mother, while feeling concerned for her children's well-being, should also remind herself that you cannot protect your children forever and that sometimes they have to learn through their own mistakes; in that sense, Ida's overprotectiveness is actually doing more harm than good if she keeps trying to meddle with Helen's business. Besides, from a sheer pragmatic viewpoint, if Helen is truly in love with Frank, by now it is too late to do anything much about it, no matter how good or bad Frank may be; by persisting in this kind of attitude, Ida can only bring about a crisis which will be painful and upsetting for all those involved. Finally, it seems to me that Ida is subconsciously trying to prevent her daughter from falling in love (or having a relationship) at all cost. Maybe she is a single mother and Helen has come to represent her only reason for living, but in that case she would be much better off trying to deal with her own frustration and letting Helen get on with her life. We can only be thankful that all mothers are not like Ida!

2. I cannot see why people from different ethnic backgrounds should not have perfectly successful marriages. It may be difficult for parents to accept somebody from a different culture as a son- or daughter-in-law, but a positive attitude can only help the young couple. Provided neither spouse adheres to strict fundamentalist religious views, there is no reason why belonging to different ethnic groups should make for any special problems. After all, Betty Mahmoodi is the exception! Better still, a child growing up in a multicultural family gets a wonderful opportunity to get a bilingual upbringing, which can only help in later life, not to mention the breadth of experience afforded by such an environment.

It may be somewhat different for people of different social classes: love may well conquer all, but sooner or later the working-class spouse may feel overwhelmed by his in-law's condescension, while the upper-class one may be too ashamed of his working-class mate in front of his friends and relatives. This having been said, love can and does overcome many barriers, so we should not give up all hope to witness a socially ill-matched couple finding some mutually satisfying meeting ground.

Besides, if we take a strict view, all couples stem from different social and cultural backgrounds! It is up to the partners to decide whether their love for each other is strong enough to overcome the hurdles that stand in the way of their happiness.

SUJET

A. COMPÉTENCE LINGUISTIQUE

I. Écrire en toutes lettres :

1. la date : 1940. . . . .
2. le nombre : 10,722 . . . .
3. l'heure : 6.15. . . . .

II. Mettre les verbes entre parenthèses au temps et à la forme voulus :

Time . . . . (to be) when U.S. presidential campaigns . . . . (to be) all about foreign policy. Remember Nixon's secret plan to end the Vietnam war in 1968? The Iranian hostage crisis in 1980? Like Bush, Clinton . . . . (to be) an internationalist who . . . . (to believe) in a strong U.S. global presence, both economically and militarily. But any new president . . . . (must) raid the defense budget for domestic needs as soon as he . . . . (to come) into office in January.

(Adapted from Newsweek. October 19, 1992.)

As he had so often during the campaign, Bill Clinton . . . . (to make) it clear last week that his top priority as president will be rebuilding the strength of the U.S. economy.

(From Newsweek. November 16, 1992.)

*III. **Relier les propositions suivantes à l'aide des mots de liaison :** unless,* **although, whereas, in order to, while,** *de façon à obtenir des phrases cohérentes :* tandis que

He is very fond of football	He can't bear classical music
You won't find me at home	You clean the house
I'll do the shopping	Speak it fluently
His father is a famous pianist	You phone me beforehand
You must practise the language every day	His sister is keen on tennis

*IV. **Reformuler les phrases suivantes en utilisant les amorces proposées et sans en changer le sens :***

1. He has lived here all his life.
   He has lived here since. . . . .

2. The best thing for you to do is to wait and see.
   You'd . . . .

3. They are building a new bridge over the river.
   A new bridge . . . .

4. She suggested we should phone them.
   What about . . . .

5. I've never read such a bad book.
   It's. . . . .

*V. **Poser les questions suggérées par les mots soulignés :***

1. They have been living there <u>for ages</u>.
   . . . .

2. Mine is <u>the blue</u> one.
   . . . .

3. <u>Our neighbour's</u> son broke the kitchen window yesterday.
   . . . .

4. It is <u>ten miles</u> from the nearest town.
   . . . .

5. He goes hunting in the mountains <u>twice a year</u>.
   . . . .

B. COMPRÉHENSION D'UN TEXTE ÉCRIT

It was hailed as one of the great archeological finds of the century; the body of a man, believed to be 5,000 years old, perfectly preserved under sheets of glacial ice until it was discovered by hikers a year ago.

The discovery of the iceman, high on the Italian-Austrian border,
5 threw the scientific world into a flurry[1]. The remains cast a new light on
late neolithic civilisation in Europe; and everything from the man's blue
eyes and black, wavy hair to his finely cut leather clothes came under
feverish examination.

A bow and arrows[2] found nearby led some to believe he was a hunter.
10 Others thought he was a holy man who had been in the mountains com-
muning with spirits when he was caught in a blizzard and froze to death.

But now a German television team have upset the experts by saying
that the find could be an elaborate hoax.

"It is irrefutable that he is about 5,000 years old," said Dr Michael
15 Heim, head of the investigative unit at the Bavarian state television
Bayerischer Rundfunk in Munich. "But we are not convinced that this
man died up there in the ice."

Heim and his team want to know why the cell membranes of the
man's eyes were undamaged; normally they would not survive more
20 than a year in extreme cold. Why was he found with a bronze axe when
carbon dating has pinpointed his death as occurring *before* the beginning
of the bronze age? And why were all his clothes, weapons and baggage
piled up beside him?

All these questions are swept aside by Professor Konrad Spindler,
25 head of the Innsbruck University's Institute of Pre-History studies. "I do
not understand why Dr Heim appears to want to mystify the discovery
or the circumstances in which the mummy was found. We do not have
any doubts about the authenticity," he said.

But Spindler does admit it is "extraordinary" that the iceman, dubbed
30 Frozen Fritz, appears to have survived intact for thousands of years
under tons of slow-moving glacier ice before surfacing on a well-trodden walkers' route last September. "It will be at least two years before
we have all the answers," he said.

Dr Heim contends that Fritz closely resembles Egyptian mummies,
35 including one lodged in the British Museum. And he points a question-
ing finger at the celebrated Italian mountaineer and self-publicist
Reinhold Messner, who just happened to be in the vicinity when Fritz
was found. Heim says that Messner, who has previously claimed to have
seen a Yeti in the Himalayas, told journalists what kind of shoes Fritz
40 was wearing before the body had been prised[3] from the ice.

"I don't have any answers, but perhaps Mr Messner does," said Heim.
The Italian mountaineer was unavailable for comment last week – he
was climbing another peak.

Adapted from Graham Lees.

---

1. to throw into a flurry: mettre en émoi.
2. a bow and arrows: un arc et des flèches.
3. to prise: soulever à l'aide d'un levier.

• Compréhension globale

1. According to you, this text is:
   a) An extract from a detective story.
   b) A scientist's report to the British Museum.
   c) A newspaper article about a recent discovery.
   d) A philosophical essay on the authenticity of archeological discoveries.

2. Which title would you give to the text?
   a) The dangers of climbing.
   b) How long can bodies be preserved in ice?
   c) Was the Alpine iceman nothing but a joke?
   d) A controversy about Egyptian mummies.

3. The passage deals with :
   a) The difficulties of finding evidence from the past.
   b) A mummy stolen from the British Museum.
   c) An amazing discovery.

• Compréhension approfondie

I. Right or wrong? Circle the letter W or R. Justify your answer by quoting from the text.

1. The 5,000-year-old body of a man was discovered in the Alpine mountains a year ago.   R - W

   . . . .

2. The body was found by a Pre-History expert.   R - W

   . . . .

3. The discovery went almost unnoticed among scientists.   R - W

   . . . .

4. All scientists agree that the iceman was a hunter.   R - W

   . . . .

5. His death was caused by an arrow that was shot at him.   R - W

   . . . .

6. Some people find the whole story hard to believe.   R - W

   . . . .

7. Scientists found out that the man's name was "Frozen Fritz".   R - W

   . . . .

8. The Italian mountaineer Messner says the man may have been a Yeti coming from the Himalayas.   R - W

   . . . .

9. The mystery won't be solved shortly.   R - W

   . . . .

10. Dr Heim suspects Messner of being better informed than scientists are about the circumstances in which the body was found.

R - W

. . . .

II. Find in the text

the equivalent of:

1. a discovery:. . . . .
2. a joke: . . . .
3. happening: . . . .
4. rejected: . . . .
5. nicknamed: . . . .
6. neighbourhood:. . . . .
7. before:. . . . .

the contrary of:

1. ruined:. . . . .
2. free:. . . . .
3. falsehood: . . . .

III. Tick the right answer:

1. "A German television team have upset the experts" means:
   a) They congratulated the experts on the discovery.
   b) They made the experts feel worried and disturbed.
   c) They criticized the experts for the discovery.
2. "Carbon dating has pinpointed his death..." means:
   a) Carbon dating has shown exactly how far back in Prehistory his death can be located.
   b) Carbon dating has shown that his death was caused by pins.
   c) The body was found with carbon paper pinned on it.
3. "A holy man" means:
   a) A man who digs holes in order to bury the dead.
   b) A man dedicated to God or to a particular religion.
   c) A man looking for holly to decorate houses at Christmas.
4. "A well-trodden route" means:
   a) A footpath which is rarely walked over.
   b) A route which has been well-kept by the road-maintenance services.
   c) A route which has been walked over by a lot of people.
5. "The remains" refers to:
   a) What was left of the body.
   b) The scientists who are mainly interested in archeological discoveries.
   c) Some ruins which were found near the body.

IV. Translate from "A bow and arrows..." to "froze to death".

V. Say to which lines the following paragraph titles would correspond.

1	Doubting the authenticity of the discovery	A	"Dr Heim contends that... he was climbing another peak".
2	A mysterious climber may have the answer	B	""All these questions... before we have all the answers", he said".
3	Divided opinions about the probable occupation of the iceman	C	"It was hailed... feverish examination".
4	Portrait of a 5,000-year-old body	D	"A bow and arrows... froze to death".
5	Why should it not be plausible?	E	"But now a German television team... baggage piled up beside him".

C. EXPRESSION ÉCRITE

I. Expression semi-guidée (100-150 mots).

Two scientists discuss about the discovery of the iceman and express divergent views on it. (Use words and expressions indicating *disagreement, doubts* and *improbability, certainty* and *probability*.)

II. Expression libre (200-250 mots).

Choose one of the two following subjects.

1. Do you think searching into the past has become less useful nowadays than preparing the future of mankind?

2. What is your attitude toward the news, however amazing it may be? Give examples to support your view.

CORRIGÉS

A. *COMPÉTENCE LINGUISTIQUE*

I

1. Nineteen forty.
2. Ten thousand seven hundred and twenty-two.
3. Six fifteen.

II

was
were
is
believes
will have to
comes
made

III

1. He is very fond of football whereas his sister is keen on tennis.
2. You won't find me at home unless you phone me beforehand.
3. I'll do the shopping while you clean the house.
4. Although his father is a famous pianist, he can't bear classical music.
5. You must practise the language every day in order to speak it fluently.

IV

1. He has lived here since he was born.
2. You'd better wait and see.
3. A new bridge is being built over the river.
4. What about phoning them ?
5. It's the worst book I've ever read.

V

1. How long have they been living here ?
2. Which (one) is yours ?
3. Whose son broke the kitchen window yesterday ?
4. How far is it from the nearest town ?
5. How often does he go hunting in the mountains ?

B. COMPRÉHENSION D'UN TEXTE ÉCRIT

- **Compréhension globale**

1. c) A newspaper article about a recent discovery.
2. c) Was the Alpine iceman nothing but a joke ?
3. c) An amazing discovery.

- **Compréhension approfondie**

I

1. RIGHT
   The body of a man, believed to be 5,000 years old [was] discovered [...] a year ago [...] high on the Italian-Austrian border.
2. WRONG
   [...] discovered by hikers.
3. WRONG
   [...] it threw the scientific world into a flurry.
4. WRONG
   Others thought he was a holy man [...].
5. WRONG
   [...] he was caught in a blizzard and froze to death.
6. RIGHT
   [...] a German TV team [have said] the find could be an elaborate hoax.
7. WRONG
   [...] dubbed "Frozen Fritz".
8. WRONG
   [...] Messner, who had <u>previously</u> claimed to have seen a Yeti in the Himalayas [...].
9. RIGHT
   It will be at least two years before we have all the answers.
10. RIGHT
    [Dr Heim] points a questioning finger at [...] Messner, [who] told journalists what kind of shoes Fritz was wearing before the body had been prised from the ice.

II

1. a find. 2. a hoax. 3. occurring. 4. swept aside. 5. dubbed.
6. vicinity. 7. previously.

1. preserved 2. caught. 3. authenticity.

III

1. b) They made the experts feel worried and disturbed.
2. a) Carbon dating has shown exactly how far back in Prehistory his death can be located.
3. b) A man dedicated to God or to a particular religion.
4. c) A route which has been walked over by a lot of people.
5. a) What was left of the body.

IV

Un arc et des flèches trouvés non loin de là ont conduit certains à croire qu'il s'agissait d'un chasseur. D'autres ont pensé que c'était un saint homme qui était allé dans les montagnes pour communier avec les esprits lorsqu'il s'est fait surprendre par un blizzard et est mort de froid.

V

1. E.   2. A.   3. D.   4. C.   5. B.

C. EXPRESSION ÉCRITE

I. Expression semi-guidée

1 = First scientist.   2 = Second scientist.

1: Do you think Frozen Fritz is genuine ?

2: He must be. How could anybody have taken him all the way up there ?

1: You never know. I don't trust this Rudolf Messner. I wonder if the whole thing might not be some huge set-up for the sake of self-publicity.

2: Even then, you have to admit the body is five thousand years old.

1: They might have faked the results.

2: Aren't you being oversuspicious ? And besides, you couldn't very well move that kind of mummy around without damaging it, so surely the body was found in the near vicinity.

1: Yes, it must have, but it may also have been some poor old shepherd whose corpse they dragged up into the ice.

2: Now that's really macabre !

II. Expression libre

1. It may seem a trifle absurd, as we stand on the threshold of the twenty-first century with threats of starvation, war and killer diseases all around us, to keep searching into the past. Should so much state money be devoted to archaelogy and paleontology when it could just as reasonably be invested into ecological and medical research? Then again, if we take this line, we could not account for most of contemporary research, dealing as it does with abstractions far removed from our basic survival. On the other hand, such arcane concerns may well turn out to give us the clue to the problems of the Third World or the AIDS epidemic, to take but two of the most pressing issues bearing on mankind today. Indeed, if I were in charge of the budget for world research, I would be hard put to decide what to subsidize. I would definitely focus on the areas I have already mentioned, but who am I to decide that this lab or that is perfectly useless? Moreover, there is more to research than just material findings: learning more about the past of mankind may well teach us a few lessons concerning the future: for example, Vernant's or Foucault's work on European antiquity is quite relevant to modern mankind, inasmuch as it forces us to rethink political, social and ethical categories. The opposition between past and future may well be a superficial one which vanishes when dealing with fundamentals as research does.

2. Without being a news freak, I am quite interested in reading papers or listening to the radio news. I have rarely come across a truly astonishing piece of news, but that may be purely because I do not read *News of the World!* However, I can remember reading about the famous corn field rings a few years ago and almost instantly deciding it was a hoax. For one thing, it was too good to be true, and it was too reminiscent of the Nazca drawings (as yet unaccounted for) to be genuine. It did eventually turn out to be an elaborate put-up job. More generally, I know the media are only too keen to publicize any kind-of sensational information for the sake of selling more issues, so I try to keep a healthy dose of scepticism towards anything too farfetched. I also try to apply this principle to matters as mundane as home or foreign politics, because I do not really trust the impartiality of the press. Ideally, if I had enough time on my hands, I would try to read several newspapers every day but this is just impossible. Instead, I try to use my own critical sense and to discuss the news with people whose opinion I trust. We live in a world where information is rapidly turning into white noise, so the only way for the media to catch our attention is to come up with ever more improbable or alluring items. The only sensible attitude is to scan the news in order to sort the grain from the chaff.

SUJET

A. COMPÉTENCE LINGUISTIQUE

I. Mettez le verbe entre parenthèses au temps et à la forme nécessaires :

1. You'd better . . . . her, otherwise she might be hurt. (to tell)

2. He should . . . . harder, he would have had a better chance of passing his exam. (to work)

3. Jane said she would phone us as soon as she . . . .(to arrive)

4. She . . . . in England for 5 years in the fifties. (to live)

5. Nobody will ever make me . . . . if I don't want to. (to sing)

II. Mettez au passif sans exprimer le complément d'agent :

1. They will tell her what to do.

. . . .

2. All the pupils laughed at him because of his hat.

. . . .

3. Some people have seen her in London.

. . . .

4. John is repairing my car, so I can't go with you.

. . . .

5. I think she could have stopped him.

. . . .

III.' Reformulez les phrases suivantes en gardant le sens et en utilisant l'amorce donnée :

1. Did you meet him in Paris?
   They asked me . . . .
2. If you had come earlier you would have seen him.
   Had . . . .
3. It's years since I saw him.
   I haven't . . . .
4. John will certainly be late because he drives very slowly.
   Since . . . .
5. It's the best book I've ever read.
   I've never . . . .

II. Complétez avec le modal le plus approprié :

   need - must - might - could - can't.

1. The lights are on, they . . . . be back.
2. I don't know, he . . . . come.
3. You . . . . not panic, it's not that terrible.
4. She . . . . have told me before.
3. Where is she? I . . . . tell you, I don't know.

V. Mettez au discours DIRECT :

1. She said she'd never tell him the truth.
   She said: " . . . . ".
2. He asked her if she'd liked the film.
   He asked her: " . . . . ".
3. He told her to shut the door.
   He said: ". . . . . ".
4. He told him he should drive more carefully.
   He said: ". . . . . ".
5. He asked her whether she loved him.
   He asked her: " . . . . ".

VI. Reliez les 2 éléments de phrase à l'aide des mots ci-dessous. Écrire la phrase complète sur la ligne suivante :

   although - since - whereas - yet - provided
   (chaque mot ne sera employé qu'une seule fois).

1. She will go to John's party   – she is seriously ill.

. . . .

2. He is very clever   – he fails all his exams.
. . . .

3. She can't marry him   – she is only 15.
. . . .

4. I'll go with you   – I'm back by ten.
. . . .

5 She never wrote to us   – her brother kept in touch for a while.
. . . .

VII. Posez la question correspondant à l'élément souligné.

1. He plays tennis <u>twice a week</u>.
. . . . ?

2. It's only <u>a few miles away</u>.
. . . . ?

3. I'd like <u>the blue</u> one, not the red one.
. . . . ?

4. He usually played tennis with <u>Jennifer</u>.
. . . . ?

5. I used that brush <u>to paint the wall</u>.
. . . . ?

VIII. Complétez avec une préposition, une particule adverbiale ou ensemble Ø.

1. I'm looking forward . . . . seeing Jim at Christmas.
2. They fight all day long and shout . . . . each other.
3. Leave a message if I'm not at home when you phone, I'll call you
. . . .
4. Are you really interested . . . . that boy?
5. Who is responsible . . . . this mess?

IX. Complétez par un "question tag".

1. People don't like him, ... ?
2. Everybody thought he was mad, ... ?
3. He never turned up, ... ?
4. Let's go to the movies, ... ?
5. That's enough, stop talking . . . . ?

THE MURDERER

"I'm here to help you," said the psychiatrist, frowning. Something was wrong with the room. He had hesitated the moment he entered. He glanced around. The prisoner laughed. "If you're wondering why it's so quiet in here, I just kicked the radio to death."

5 Violent, thought the doctor.

The prisoner read this thought, smiled, put out a gentle hand. "No, only to machines that yak-yak-yak."

Bits of the wall radio's tubes and wires lay on the grey carpeting. Ignoring these, feeling that smile upon him like a heat lamp, the psy-

10 chiatrist sat across from his patient in the unusual silence which was like the gathering of a storm.

"You're Mr Albert Brock, who calls himself The Murderer?"

Brock nodded pleasantly. "Before we start..." He moved quietly and quickly to detach the wrist radio from the doctor's arm. He tucked it in

15 teeth like a walnut, gritted, heard it crack, handed it back to the appalled psychiatrist as if he had done them both a favour. "That's better."

The psychiatrist stared at the ruined machine. "Shall we start?" he said.

"Fine. The first victim, or one of the first, was my telephone. Murder

20 most foul. Poor thing strangled to death. After that I shot the television set!"

The psychiatrist said, "Mmm."

"Fired six shots right through the cathode."

"Suppose you tell me, when you first began to hate the telephone."

25 "It frightened me as a child. Uncle of mine called it the Ghost Machine. Voices without bodies. Scared the living hell out of me. Later in life I was never comfortable. Seemed to me a phone was an impersonal instrument.

"It's easy to say the wrong thing on telephones; the telephone changes

30 your meaning on you. First thing you know, you've made an enemy. Then, of course, the telephone's such a convenient thing; it just sits there and demands you call someone who doesn't want to be called. Friends were always calling, calling, calling me. Hell, I hadn't any time of my own. When it wasn't the telephone it was the television, the radio, or the

35 phonograph. When it wasn't the television or radio or phonograph it was motion pictures at the corner theatre, motion pictures projected with commercials, music by Mozzek in every restaurant; music and commercials on the buses I rode to work. When it wasn't music, it was interoffice communications, and my horror chamber of a radio wristwatch on

40 which my friends and my wife phoned every five minutes.

I love my friends, my wife, humanity, very much, but when one minute my wife calls to say, "Where are you now, dear?" and a friend calls and says, "Got the best off-colour joke to tell you." Well... then I got the idea at noon of stamping my wrist radio on the sidewalk. Then do you

45 know what I did, Doctor? I bought a quart of French chocolate ice
cream and spooned it into the car radio transmitter."
   "What made you think of spooning ice cream into the radio?"
   "It was a hot day."
   The doctor paused.
50 "And what happened next?"
   "Silence happened next. God, it was beautiful!"

Adapted from Ray Bradbury. *Short Stories.*

● **Compréhension globale**

*I. Circle the most appropriate answer and justify by quoting from the text
(line 1 to 18):*

1. Where is Mr. Albert Brock?
   a) in an asylum.
   b) in hospital.
   c) in jail.
   . . . .

2. Mr. Albert Brock can't stand:
   a) radios' tubes and wires.
   b) cathodes.
   c) everything that makes a noise.
   . . . .

3. The attitude of Albert Brock towards the psychiatrist is:
   a) violent.
   b) threatening.
   c) courteous.
   . . . .

4. The psychiatrist is:
   a) horrified.
   b) amused.
   c) indifferent.
   . . . .

5. This passage is mainly about:
   a) the difficulty of working in a hospital.
   b) violence in our society.
   c) the aggressions of modern life.
   . . . .

● **Compréhension approfondie**

*I. Mr. Albert Brock calls himself <u>The Murderer.</u> Pick out five expressions
referring to "his crimes".*

   . . . .
   . . . .

II. RIGHT or WRONG. Write R or W in the box and justify by quoting from the text.

1. The psychiatrist "had hesitated the moment he entered" because he thought the prisoner was violent.

   ☐ ....

2. The prisoner's laugh made the psychiatrist feel warm and comfortable.

   ☐ ....

3. He considered it was a good thing for the psychiatrist and for himself to have broken the doctor's wrist radio.

   ☐ ....

4. His uncle called the telephone the ghost machine because you can't see the person you are talking to.

   ☐ ....

5. He destroyed his wrist radio by spooning ice cream into it.

   ☐ ....

III. Find an equivalent in the text for:

1. showed his agreement (line 6 → 30) ....
2. frightened to death (line 6 → 30) ....
3. handy (line 30 → 40) ....
4. movie (line 30 → 40) ....
5. pavement (line 30 → 44) ....

C. EXPRESSION PERSONNELLE

I. Production semi-guidée (150 words).

Back home the psychiatrist tells a colleague about his new patient Mr. Albert Brock. You will use phrases expressing: contrast, purpose, surprise. You will also use some reported speech. Underline the relevant elements.

II. Production libre (200/250 words).

Traitez un des deux sujets suivants :

1. Noise: a major sort of pollution. Would you agree?
2. What do you find physically or mentally unbearable in life? Explain why.

CORRIGÉS

A. *COMPÉTENCE LINGUISTIQUE*

I

1. tell.
2. have worked.
3. arrived.
4. lived.
5. sing.

II

1. She will be told what to do.
2. He was laughed at because of his hat.
3. She has been seen in London.
4. My car is being repaired, so I can't go with you.
5. I think he could have been stopped.

III

1. They asked me whether if I had met him in Paris.
2. Had you come earlier, you would have seen him.
3. I haven't seen him for years/in years.
4. Since John drives very slowly, he will certainly be late.
5. I've never read such a good book.

IV

1. must.
2. might.
3. need.
4. could.
5. can't.

V

1. I'll never tell him the truth.
2. Did you like the film ?
3. Shut the door !
4. You should drive more carefully.
5. Do you love me ?

VI

1. She will go to John's party although she is seriously ill.
2. He is very clever; yet, he fails all his exams.
3. She can't marry him since she is only 15.
4. I'll go with you provided I'm back by ten.
5. She never wrote to us whereas her brother kept in touch for a while.

VII

1. How often does he play tennis?
2. How far is it?
3. Which one would you like?
4. Who did he usually play tennis with?
5. What did you use that brush for?

VIII

1. to.
2. at.
3. back.
4. in.
5. for.

IX

1. do they?
2. didn't they?
3. did he?
4. shall we?
5. will you?

B. COMPRÉHENSION D'UN TEXTE ÉCRIT

● **Compréhension globale**

I

1. a) in an asylum (he is visited by a psychiatrist), or c) in jail (he is referred to as "the prisoner"). Better still, he must be in some kind of psychiatric hospital.
2. c) everything that makes a noise.
   "No, only to machines that yak-yak-yak."

3. c) courteous.
   The prisoner [...] put out a gentle hand.
   Brock nodded pleasantly.
4. a) horrified.
   [...] the appalled psychiatrist.
5. c) the aggressions of modern life (if you consider the whole text),
   or a) the difficulty of working in a hospital (if you restrict yourself to lines 1 to 11):
   [...] the psychiatrist sat across from his patient in the unusual
   silence which was like the gathering of a storm.

• **Compréhension approfondie**

I

1. I just <u>kicked</u> the radio <u>to death</u>.
2. The first <u>victim</u> was my telephone.
3. <u>Murder</u> most foul.
4. Poor thing <u>strangled to death</u>.
5. After that I <u>shot</u> the television set.
6. <u>Fired six shots</u> right through the cathode.
7. [...] <u>stamping</u> my wrist radio on the sidewalk.

II

1. WRONG
   Something was wrong with the room.
2. WRONG
   Violent, thought the doctor.
3. RIGHT
   "That's better."
4. RIGHT
   Voices without bodies.
5. WRONG
   [...] spooned it into <u>the car radio transmitter</u>.

III

1. nodded.
2. scared the living hell out of me.
3. convenient.
4. motion picture.
5. sidewalk.

C. EXPRESSION PERSONNELLE

I. Expression semi-guidée

<u>You should have seen</u> the raving loonie they sent me out to examine today! His name's Alfred Brock and he has a thing about electrical appliances that talk. He kept telling me these horror stories about murdering telephones and wrist radios, he <u>even</u> crunched mine to death. <u>I couldn't believe it</u>. <u>Funny thing is</u>, he's <u>otherwise</u> as meek as a lamb. Just another case of social maladjustment, I suppose. He even <u>told me he's spooned</u> a quart of chocolate ice cream down his car radio. He <u>said he called</u> the Ghost Machine on the phone . <u>Can you imagine</u>? Anyway, it sounds as if he had a phobia of disembodied voices. I'm seeing him again tomorrow, <u>I'll try to</u> get him to tell me about his relatives.

II. Expression libre

1. Noise may be the worst form of pollution for it is the most insidious. Whereas you simply cannot breathe if the air is thick with industrial fumes or car exhausts, you can adjust deceptively well to the level of noise around you. The lack of any immediate reaction such as coughing does not make noise any the less harmful: it has been proved scientifically that regular exposure to noise which exceeds eighty decibels can cause serious health problems such as involuntary muscular contractions, intestinal problems and loss of balance, and eventually deafness. Things rarely go that far, but it is surely a cause for concern.

Indeed, I wonder what listening to music on a personal stereo for any length of time can do to your body. I pity those poor zombie-like souls you meet on public transport, completely absorbed in the heavy metal riffs clattering through their headphones. True, I do listen to loud music myself occasionally, but I never do so for very long, and only when in a particularly foul mood!

Worse still, you may have noisy neighbours. Although there are regulations strictly limiting the level of noise you may rightfully accept from the people next-door, it is actually a very awkward situation to deal with. Should you go and tell your neighbours directly, and find they have actually turned the volume *up* by the time you get back to your flat? Or should you call the police straight away and run the risk of finding rubbish in your letter-box the next day? All in all, it may be much ado about nothing...

2. There are so many odd little things I find unbearable in life that I would rather not start drawing a list of all my private phobias, from wet sponges to alarm clocks! But the thing I find most unbearable of all, commonplace as it may sound, is pain in any form. I do not like physical pain, although I know that I can withstand it quite stolidly. It is not that I am afraid of it but it just seems so useless: if a tooth is giving me trouble, I know I have to go the dentist's. Why can't the vile thing stop hurting the minute I have made my appointment? I am going to have it seen to, so why can't it behave and leave me alone until the day of the appointment? Yet there is one thing worse than physical pain, and that is mental pain. It seems even more useless than the physical kind because there is so little to be done about it except grin and bear it. Heartaches for example seem like a complete waste of time: you know (or if *you* do not, the people around you *do* know) that it can only get better, whether you patch up with whoever made you unhappy in the first place or whether you eventually forget about them. What's the good of having suffered like an early Christian martyr in the meantime? Some people say that suffering ultimately makes you a better kind of person, I can only hope it is true because I really cannot see any other justification for it.

LISTES PRATIQUES

- **Link words and useful expressions**
- **How to express…**

LINK WORDS...

consequence

- consequently, therefore, as a result
- so... that, so long as *(du moment que)*, all the more... as *(d'autant plus... que)*, as

cause

- thus *(ainsi)*, owing to, *(en raison de)*
- the reason why, because, since *(puisque)*, for *(car)*

concession, opposition

- though, although *(bien que, quoique)*, even though *(même si)*, as though *(comme si)*
- in spite of/despite *(malgré, en dépit de)*, still, yet *(pourtant, cependant - en début de phrase)*, on the contrary, actually *(en fait)*, no matter what/where/who *(quoi/où/qui que ce soit)*
- however/nevertheless

condition

- if, unless *(à moins que)*, as long as/provided/providing that *(pourvu que)*, whether... or *(que... ou que)*
- or else/otherwise *(sinon - condition négative)*

result

- so as to/so that/in order to/in order that *(pour que)*
- so/as a result

time

- when, whenever, as, as soon as, no sooner... than/hardly... when *(pas plus tôt/à peine... que)*

- before, after, since *(depuis)*, for *(depuis, pendant)*, until, while, in the meantime/meanwhile *(pendant ce temps/entre-temps)*

fear

- for fear that *(de crainte que)*, lest + subj. + should *(de peur que)*

restriction

- whereas *(tandis que)*, not that *(non pas que)*
- however + adj. *(bien que)*, however *(cependant)*, unlike + noun *(contrairement à)*, nevertheless *(néanmoins)*, all the same *(malgré tout)*

addition, enumeration

- first of all, to begin with, in the first place, first and foremost *(en tout premier lieu)*, for one thing/on the one hand *(d'abord/d'une part)*, for another thing/on the other hand *(d'autre part)*
- thus *(ainsi)*, therefore, besides *(en outre)*, in addition, moreover/furthermore/what is more *(de plus/du reste)*
- last, finally, to conclude/to sum up, as a conclusion, in a word, to put it in a nutshell *(en un mot)*, eventually *(finalement)*

hypothesis

- in case *(au cas où)*, suppose/supposing *(à supposer que)*

...AND USEFUL EXPRESSIONS

— to weigh the pros and cons *(peser le pour et le contre)*
— all things considered *(toute réflexion faite)*
— in every respect *(à tous égards)*
— in other words
— to tell the truth *(à vrai dire)*
— if need be *(le cas écheant)*
— at any rate, anyway
— so to speak, up to a point, that is to say
— to some/a certain extent
— significantly enough

— by all/no means
— similarly *(de la même manière)*, equally
— needless to say that
— from time immemorial *(depuis toujours)*
— as a matter of fact, by the way
— incidentally *(à propos - when interrupting someone)*
— I say *(dites donc)*
— with the exception of
— for example/instance, such as, including

HOW TO EXPRESS...

REGRET

— What a pity/shame he isn't here! *(quel dommage...)*
— How stupid of me to have missed the train!
— If only I had gone for a walk/I should have gone for a walk.
— I regret what I have done.
— I was wrong.
— I wish I could have gone on holiday.
— Why did(n't) I go with my friends?
— If I had known, I would(n't) have insisted!

HOPE/WISH

— I hope/hopefully/let's hope we'll meet again.
— I'm looking forward to seeing you.
— I can't wait until we meet again.
— I keep hoping you'll come soon.
— I wish/want/would like to visit Egypt.
— It would be nice/great to play tennis.

APPROVAL/DISAPPROVAL

— I think so/I don't think so.
— I agree/disagree with you.
— I go along with what you said.
— I am of the same opinion/I have a different opinion.
— I approve/disapprove of it.
— It's exactly what I think.
— That's my point of view.
— I can't agree more.
— I share the same views as you.
— You are mistaken. *(Tu te trompes.)*
— You're right/wrong.
— I'd like to correct you there.

ANGER / EXASPERATION

— I'm furious / steaming!
— I'm tired of/fed up with their shouting.
— I have had enough of it!
— I can't stand it/put up with it (*supporter*)!
— I won't have it (*Je ne permettrai pas ça*)!
— There is no reason why I should stand it!
— I can't take any more of it!
— What gets on my nerves is…
— That's the last straw! (*C'est le comble !*)
— I'm warning you! (*Je te préviens !*)
— She drives me mad.
— Control yourself!
— I'm losing my temper.
— Don't create an uproar! Don't make a fuss about it.
— to shout/scream at someone; to have a row/an argument with someone.
— I want to get it over with you (*en finir avec quelqu'un*).

PERSONAL OPINION

— I think / feel / suppose / consider that…
— It seems to me that…
— In my view/opinion…
— To my mind/From my point of view/As far as I am concerned…
— My view is that…(*mon avis est que…*)
— I do believe/I am aware that…
— What I mean is…

APOLOGIZING

— I'm very / so / awfully / extremely sorry.
— I apologize for being late.
— Excuse my being late.
— Pardon me! (*Mille pardons !*)

— I had no intention or arriving late.
— I didn't do it on purpose (*exprès*).
— Forgive me for what I said.
— I didn't mean to disappoint you.

LIKES / DISLIKES / PREFERENCE

— I like / enjoy / love / dislike / hate music/playing the piano.
— I am keen on/fond of reading.
— It pleases me to have long hair.
— I can't stand/bear (*supporter*) doing nothing.
— I am interested in playing the violin.
— I am good/no good at playing tennis.
— I am hopeless (*nul*) at playing chess.
— My hobby/favourite occupation is reading.
— I'd rather read.
— I'd like/prefer to read.
— My parents would rather I were a musician/would prefer me to be a musician.

UNCERTAINTY/DOUBT

— He must be a tourist.
— It might be difficult.
— It's difficult to say for certain/It is likely that…
— It is reported that she might have been delayed.
— I can't take for granted what you said.
— I am not quite sure/I can't say for sure.
— It's doubtful that it may rain.
— It looks as if it were going to rain.
— I wish I could be sure about it.
— He seems/looks/sounds pleased.
— There is (some) reason to believe he won't come.
— I wonder if I will like it.

FEAR/ANXIETY

— I am worried/anxious/upset about.
— I am thoroughly terrified of coming home alone.
— I am afraid/scared/frightened.
— I am absolutely panic-stricken.
— I am scared stiff *(J'ai une peur bleue)*.
— I worry a lot about my family.
— I can feel my heart pounding in my throat.
— It's nightmarish/a nightmare.
— I shudder at the thought that... *(frissonner)*
— I am thrilled/restless *(agité)*

CONTRAST/COMPARISON

— However intelligent he might be... *(Si intelligent qu'il soit...)*
— And yet/but/whereas/unlike/although.
— The more you run, the more exhausted you'll be.
— He is more and more tired.
— To compare to *(comparer à)*/to compare with *(se comparer à)*.

SURPRISE/PLEASURE/ EXCLAMATION

— How surprising/astonishing/amazing that you should arrive tomorrow !
— Isn't it incredible that you should be my cousin!
— I'm amazed/flabbergasted/surprised at it!
— I can't believe my ears/eyes!
— I can hardly believe it!
— I am fascinated/dumbfounded/spellbound/under a spell/so excited!
— I am lost in wonder.
— I am speechless/shocked about it!
— How in the world/on earth did he do that?
— How is such a thing possible?
— I would never have thought that...
— You must be joking/kidding/pulling my leg!
— I am so glad/pleased/happy/overjoyed/delighted.
— What a beautiful evening! *(what + a/an + dénombrable singulier)*
— What courage he has! *(what + indénombrable singulier)*
— What beautiful evenings we used to spend! *(what + dénombrable pluriel)*

REPROACH

— You are responsible/to blame for it.
— How can/could you do such a villainy?
— It's all your fault.
— Why on earth did you...
— She should/shouldn't invite/have invited them.
— How dare you say such a thing? *(Comment oses-tu...?)*
— If only you had arrived earlier!
— I accuse you of pretending... *(de faire semblant)*

LISTES DES TEXTES PROPOSÉS

RELEVÉ DES POINTS DE GRAMMAIRE

(les chiffres renvoient aux numéros des pages où se trouvent les exercices)

adjectifs possessifs et pronoms
70, 80

articles
18, 90

discours direct
140

discours indirect
71, 111, 121, 140

forme interrogative
39, 141

formes verbales : temps et aspects
9, 10, 18, 19, 39, 40, 59, 60, 80, 92, 101, 111, 120, 121, 129, 139

lexique
9, 19, 30, 60, 81, 112

modaux
50, 60, 101, 111, 140

mots de liaison et relatifs
19, 39, 49, 59, 60, 71, 101, 111, 129, 140

multiples
31, 40, 49, 50, 60, 70, 81, 91, 100, 112, 120, 130, 140

phonétique
30, 70, 90

prépositions
90, 141

question tags
71, 121, 141

GROUPEMENT D'ACADÉMIES

- **Groupement I**

Amiens
Lille
Rouen

} même sujet que Arcueil (Paris-Créteil-Versailles)

- **Groupement II**

Bordeaux
Caen
Clermont-Ferrand
Limoges
Orléans-Tours
Poitiers
Rennes

} même sujet que Nantes

- **Groupement III**

Besancon
Dijon
Grenoble
Lyon
Nancy-Metz
Reims

} même sujet que Strasbourg

- **Groupement IV**

Aix-Marseille
Montpellier
Nice
Corse

} même sujet que Toulouse

Aubin Imprimeur

LIGUGÉ, POITIERS

Dépôt légal : août 1993
N° d'impression L 43621
Imprimé en France